Usborne

All you need to know about Your Body by age 7

Alice James

Illustrated by Stefano Tognetti

Designed by Alice Reese

Series editor: Rosie Dickins
Series designer: Zoe Wray

Experts: Dr. Caitríona Cox
and Penny Coltman

Contents

Here's a list of the different topics covered in this book.

 4   All kinds of bodies

 6   What can your body do?

 8   The outside of your body

 14   Under your skin

 16   Pumping blood

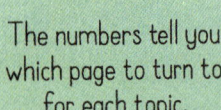

The numbers tell you which page to turn to for each topic.

 20   Breathe

 22   Munch, gurgle, plop!

 26   Your bones

 28   Busy brain

Find out more about your body at **Usborne Quicklinks.**

For links to websites where you can watch videos about the human body, discover fun facts and find activities and experiments to try at home, go to usborne.com/Quicklinks and type in the title of this book. Children should be supervised online.

 **32** Your senses

 **38** Lots of feelings

 **46** Staying healthy

 **52** Being ill

 **60** Allergies

 **62** Growing and changing

 **68** What makes you YOU

 **70** Amazing body facts

 **78** Glossary

 **80** Index

I'm a knowledge bug! Join me and my friends as we find out about your amazing body.

You can find lots of fun facts and see pictures of your main body parts here.

All kinds of bodies

Everyone has a body. Each body looks a little bit different, but they all work and grow in the same kind of way.

Bodies come in a range of heights, sizes and shapes.

Different people have different skin, different hairstyles, and wear different clothes.

We are all HUMANS.

Some people look very similar.

We're twins!

What can your body do?

So many things! Here we've grouped together some of the main ones.

MOVING AROUND

Jumping

Dancing

Running

SPLASH

Swimming

SENSING WHAT'S AROUND YOU

Smelling

Tasting

Seeing

Touching

Hearing

COMMUNICATING

Talking

LAAAA

Listening

Writing

Singing

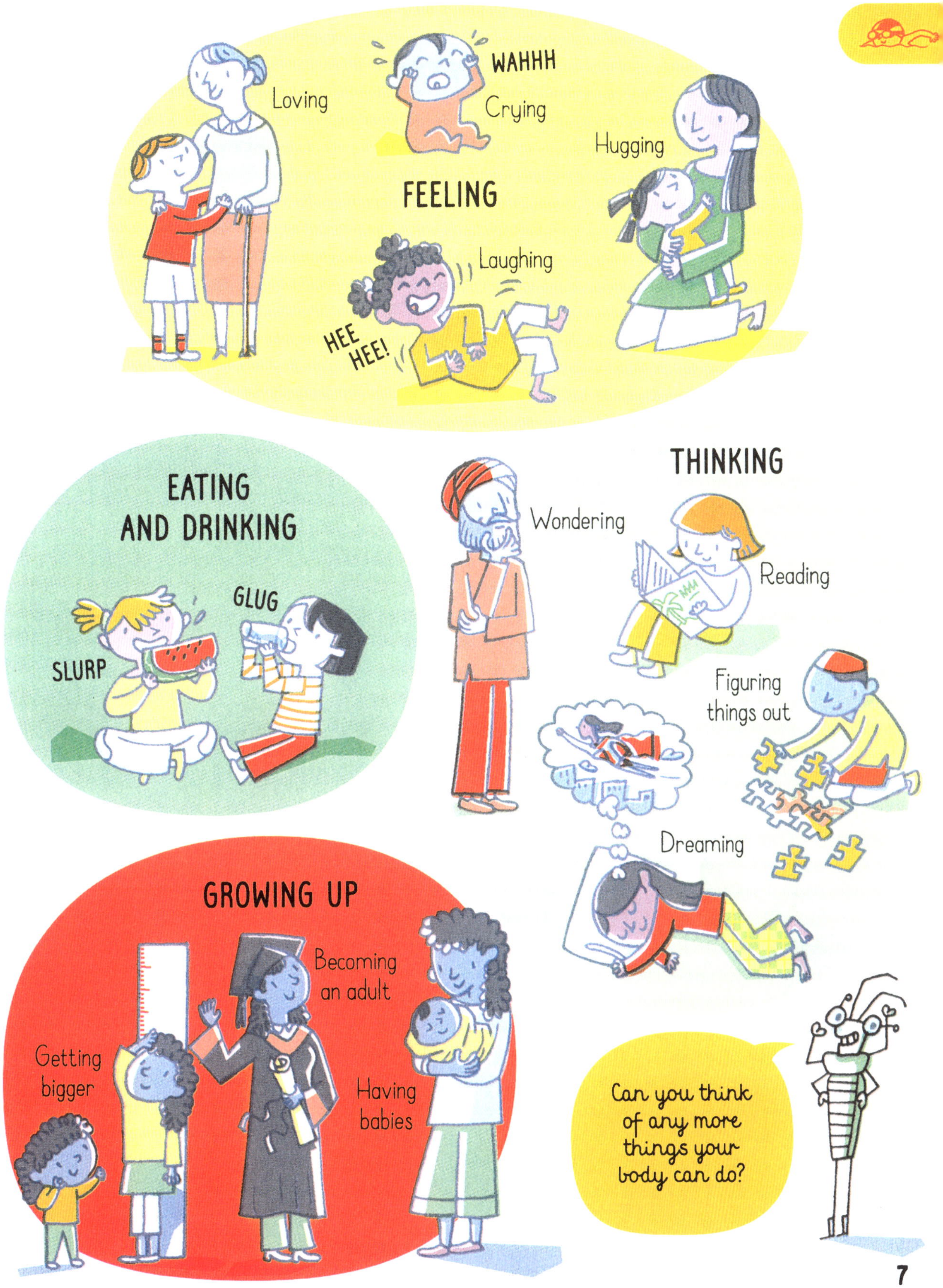
FEELING
Loving
WAHHH
Crying
Hugging
Laughing
HEE HEE!
EATING AND DRINKING
SLURP
GLUG
THINKING
Wondering
Reading
Figuring things out
Dreaming
GROWING UP
Getting bigger
Becoming an adult
Having babies
Can you think of any more things your body can do?

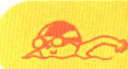

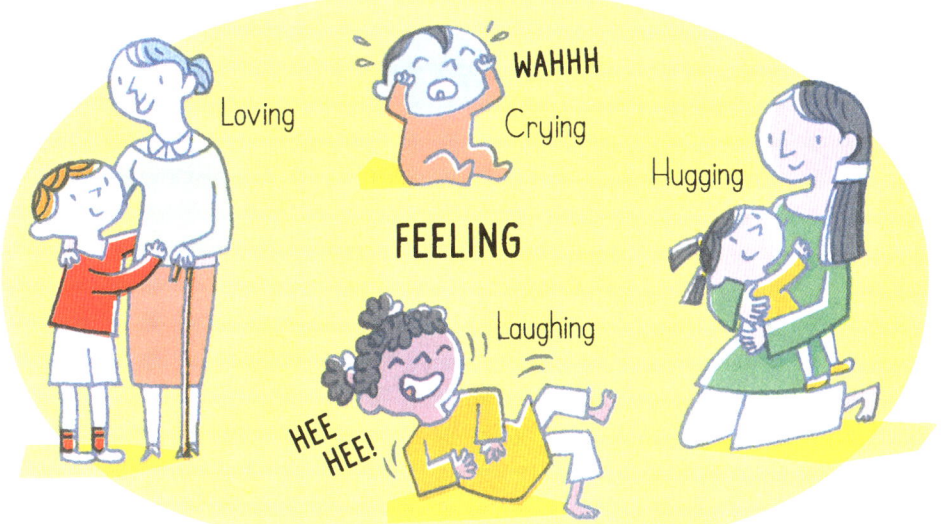

The outside of your body

On the outside, most bodies look something like this.

Here are some of your main body parts.

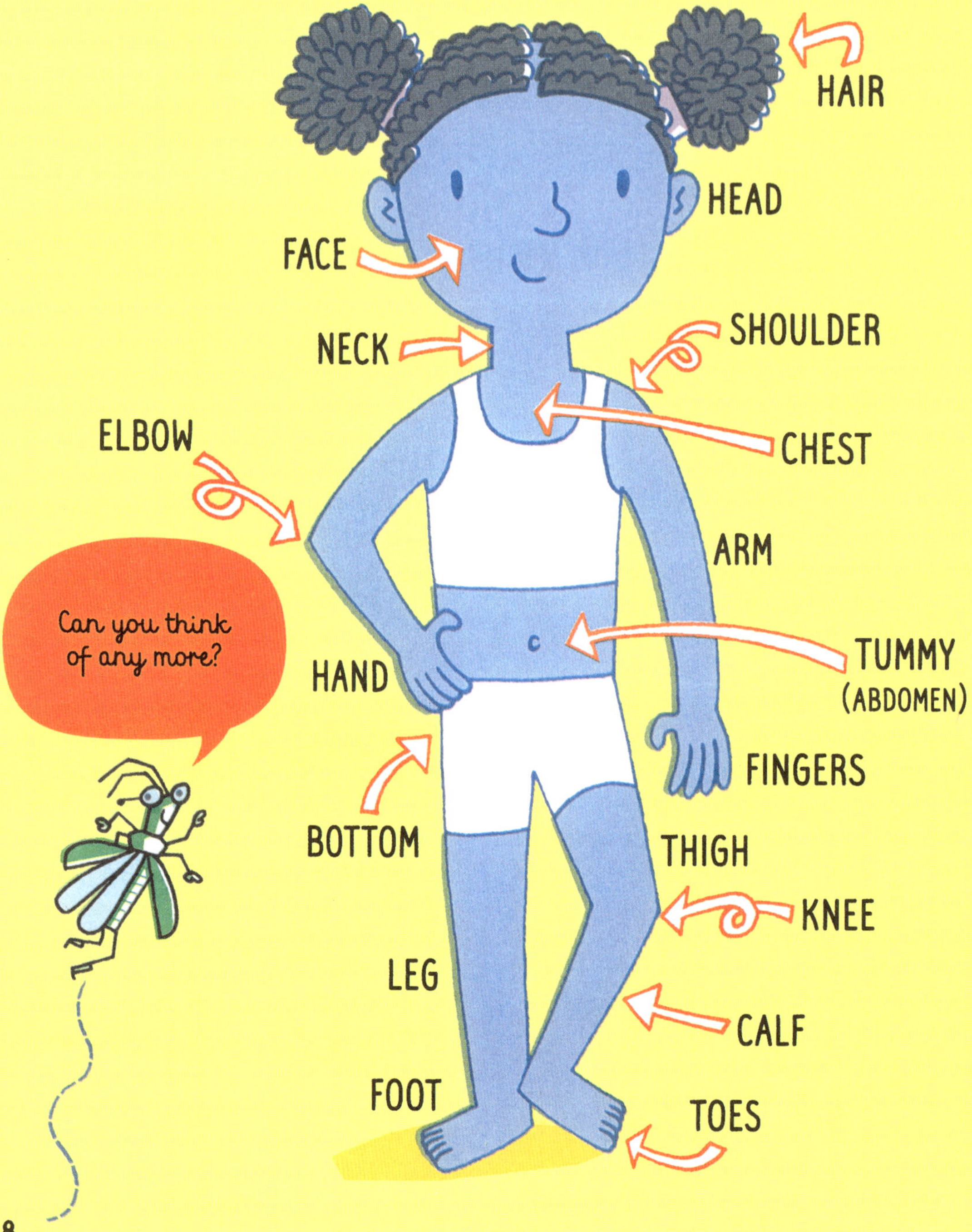

- HAIR
- HEAD
- FACE
- NECK
- SHOULDER
- ELBOW
- CHEST
- ARM
- HAND
- TUMMY (ABDOMEN)
- FINGERS
- BOTTOM
- THIGH
- KNEE
- LEG
- CALF
- FOOT
- TOES

Can you think of any more?

If you zoom in on your face, there are even more parts.

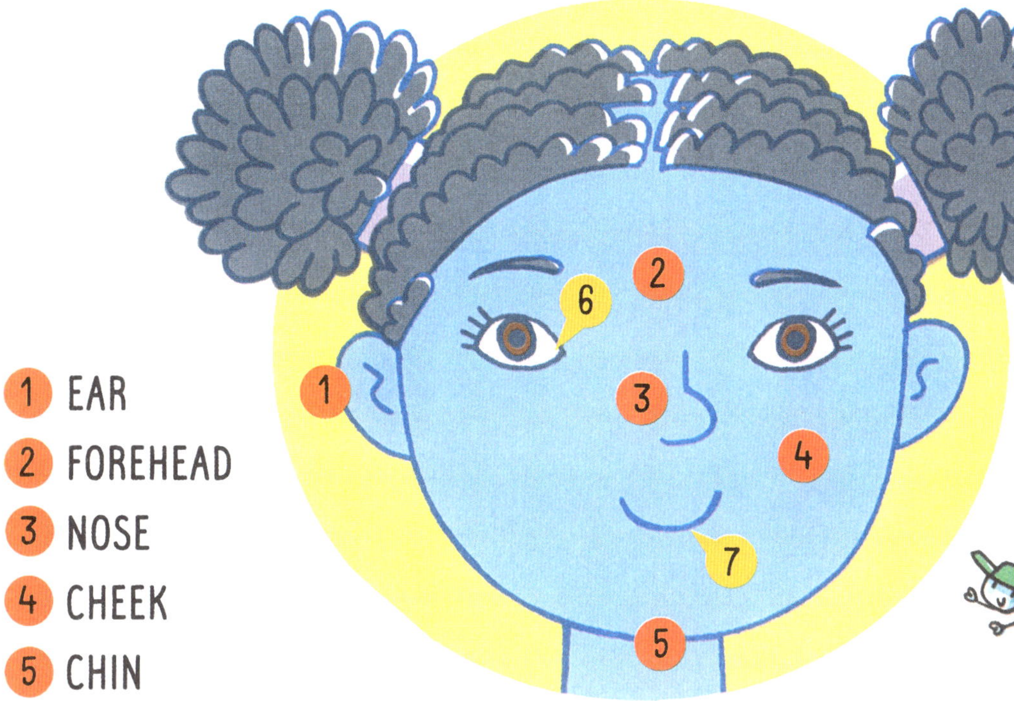

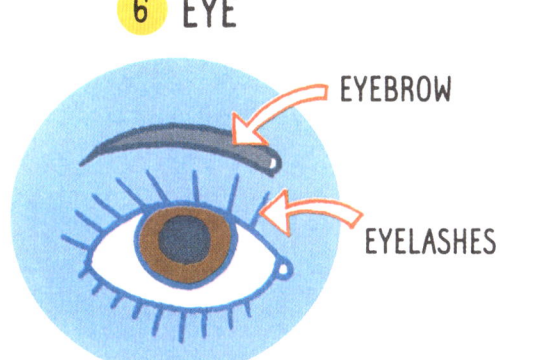

1. EAR
2. FOREHEAD
3. NOSE
4. CHEEK
5. CHIN

6. EYE
- EYEBROW
- EYELASHES

7. MOUTH
- LIPS
- TEETH
- TONGUE

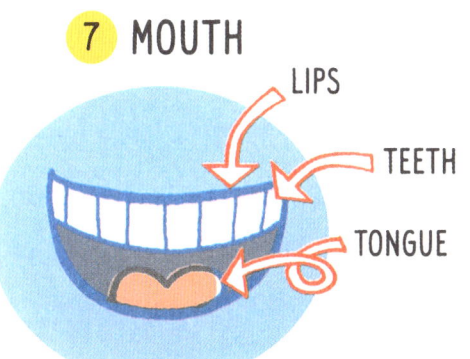

Teeth are covered in a super-tough substance called ENAMEL.

As a child you have 20 small teeth, which fall out as you grow big teeth.

By the time you're grown up you will have 32 teeth.

Your body is covered in stretchy, waterproof skin.
Your skin protects your body from the outside world.

Your skin stops dirt and germs from getting inside your body.

Tiny sensors in your skin help you to FEEL things.

Skin comes in a range of shades. That's because of a substance called MELANIN, which protects it from getting damaged by the sun. Different people have different amounts of melanin in their skin.

The darker your skin is, the more protection you have.

Whatever your skin looks like, it's sensible to cover up with clothes or sunscreen in hot sun.

Try to stay in the shade in the middle of hot, sunny days.

Your skin is special and unique to you.
It's exactly you-shaped, and it tells a story about you.

These little dots are freckles! I get more when it's sunny.

My face has lots of wrinkles. They show I've laughed a lot in my life.

This dark patch is called a birthmark. Nobody else has one quite like mine.

I've got a scar from when I had an operation.

TRY IT YOURSELF

The patterns on the end of your fingers are called FINGERPRINTS.
No one else has the same fingerprints as you – they are UNIQUE.

Use an ordinary HB pencil to scribble a patch on a piece of paper.

Rub one of your fingertips over it. Then press that finger hard onto a blank space.

Look at your prints. Can you see the patterns?

You also have unique prints on your toes.

You probably have lots of hair on your head. If you could count all the strands, there would probably be over 100,000.

Hair helps to keep the sun off your head when it's hot, and keeps your head warm when it's cold.

You also have hair on your face. Eyebrows stop sweat dripping into your eyes. Eyelashes stop dust and dirt getting to your eyes.

Some grown-ups also get hair on their chins. They can shave it off or let it grow into a beard and moustache.

Everyone's hair is a little bit different.

Hair can be short or long.

Some hair is curly and thick.

"I've just had my hair cut."

"I braid my hair."

Some hair is straight and fine.

"I brush my hair every day so it doesn't get too tangled."

Hair can be black, brown, blond, red or white...

"Red hair is quite rare. Only 1% of people in the world have it."

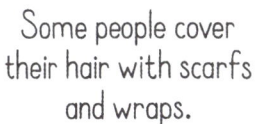

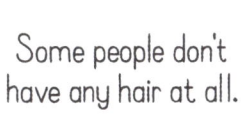

"I dye my hair blue!"

Some people cover their hair with scarfs and wraps.

Some people don't have any hair at all.

"I wear this satin bonnet at night, to protect my curly hair."

Under your skin

If you could peek underneath your skin you would see your MUSCLES. They are super-strong parts of your body, that you use to move.

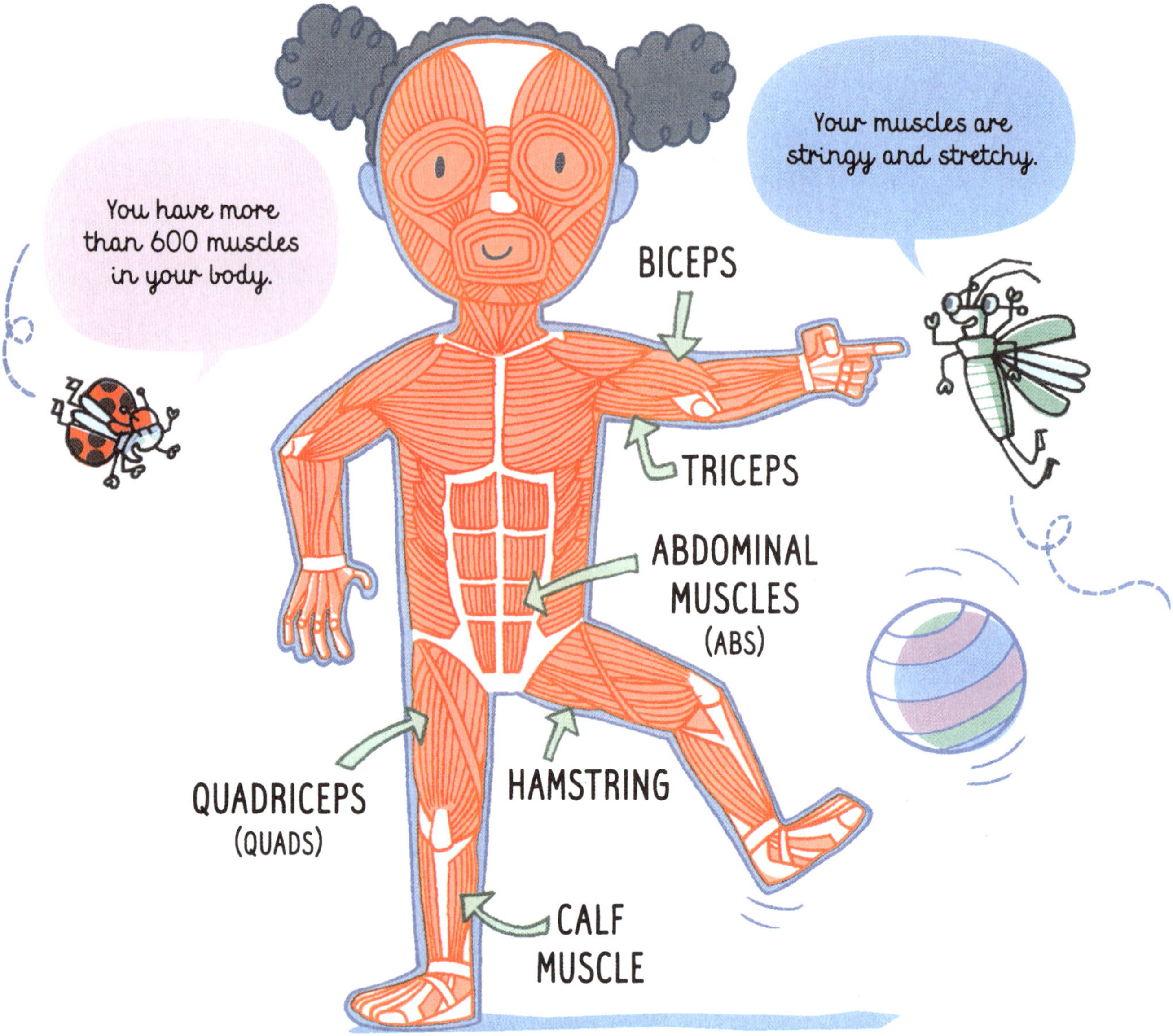

You have more than 600 muscles in your body.

Your muscles are stringy and stretchy.

BICEPS

TRICEPS

ABDOMINAL MUSCLES (ABS)

QUADRICEPS (QUADS)

HAMSTRING

CALF MUSCLE

You need muscles to...

Smile

Blink

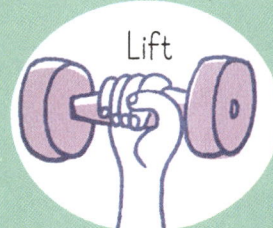
Lift

14

Most muscles work in PAIRS. When one tenses, the other relaxes.

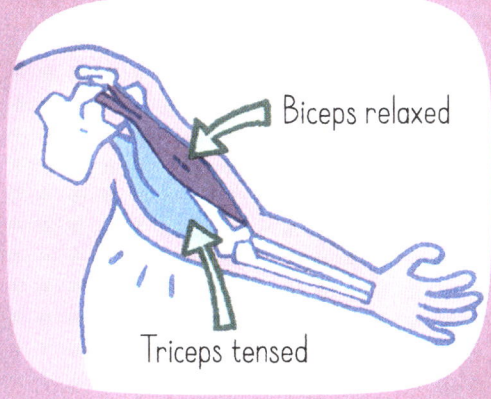

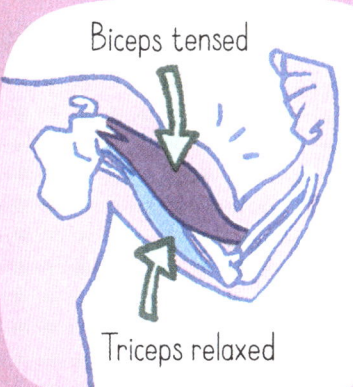

TRY IT YOURSELF

1. Put one arm out in front of you, with your hand facing up. Hold your upper arm with the other hand.

2. Bend your elbow and move your extended arm up and down, keeping your elbow still.

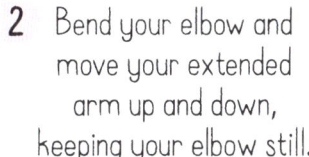

Can you feel the muscles under your hand move and change?

And to do anything else that involves movement.

Pumping blood

For your muscles to work, they need a constant supply of BLOOD. Blood carries important substances around your body.

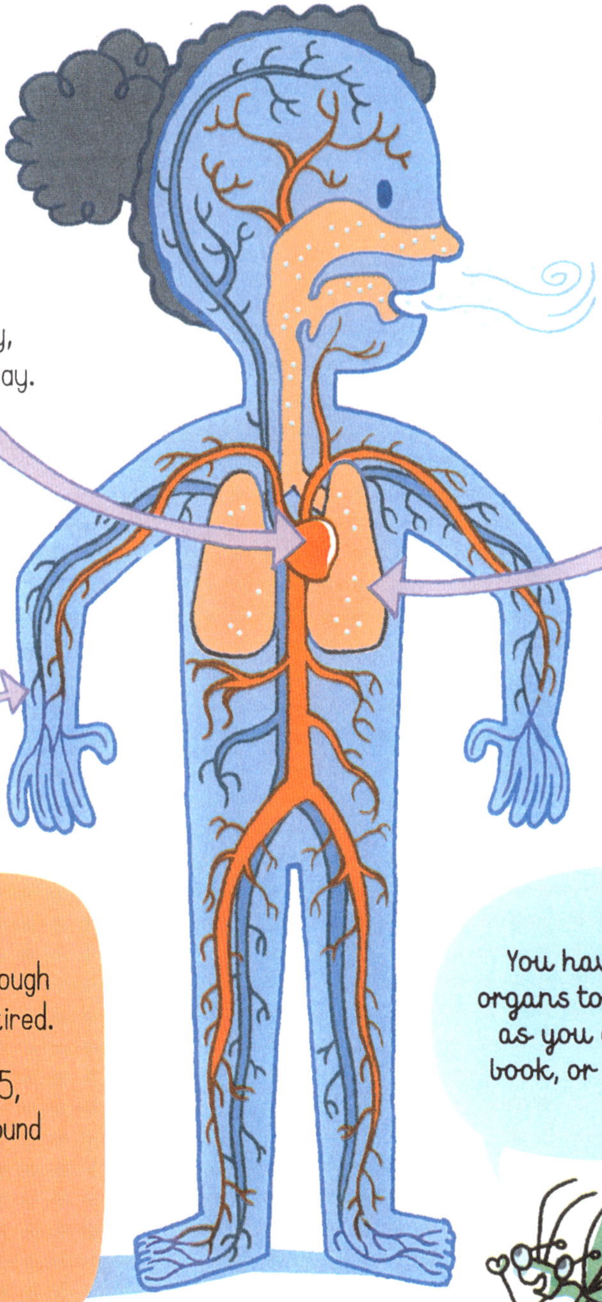

HEART
Your heart pumps blood around your body, every second of every day.

LUNGS
As your blood flows around your lungs, it collects OXYGEN – a gas in the air that you need to survive.

BLOOD VESSELS
These carry your blood around your body.

Your heart and lungs are called ORGANS.

Your heart beats all through your life and never gets tired.

If you live till you're 75, your heart will beat around 2.5 BILLION times.

You have LOTS of other organs too. You'll see more as you go through the book, or on pages 76-77.

There are three kinds of blood vessels.

ARTERIES
Arteries, shown in red, are your biggest, thickest blood vessels. They take blood AWAY from your heart.

VEINS
Veins, shown in blue, take blood BACK to your heart. They are thinner than arteries.

If you stretched out all your blood vessels, they could wrap around the world twice!

CAPILLARIES
Capillaries are tiny tubes that reach the furthest parts of you – including your fingers and toes. They join up your veins and arteries.

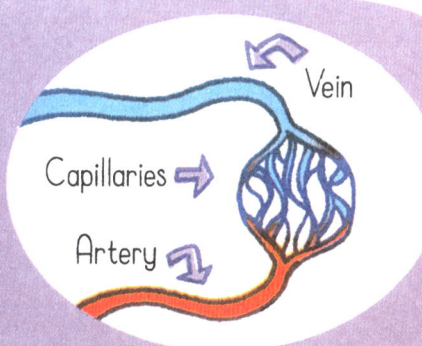

Blood is a sticky, red liquid. But if you looked at it under a microscope, you would see it's made of several different things.

RED BLOOD CELLS

Blood is red because it contains lots of little red discs called red blood cells. Red blood cells carry oxygen from your lungs around your whole body.

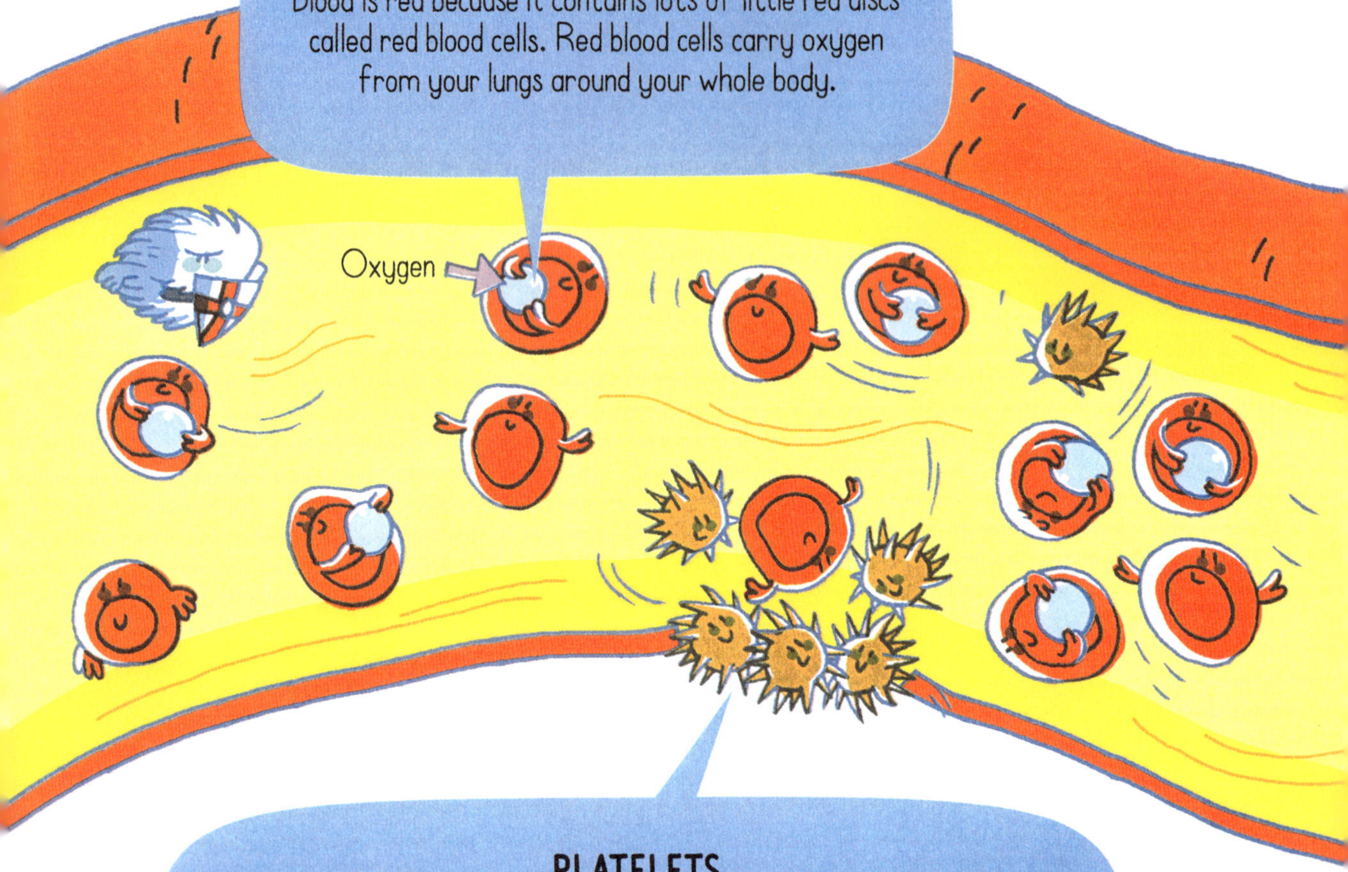

Oxygen

PLATELETS

Spiky cells called platelets help to make scabs if you cut yourself.

When you get a cut or a graze, platelets gather at the cut.

The platelets catch more blood cells, which dry out and turn into a scab. That stops germs getting in!

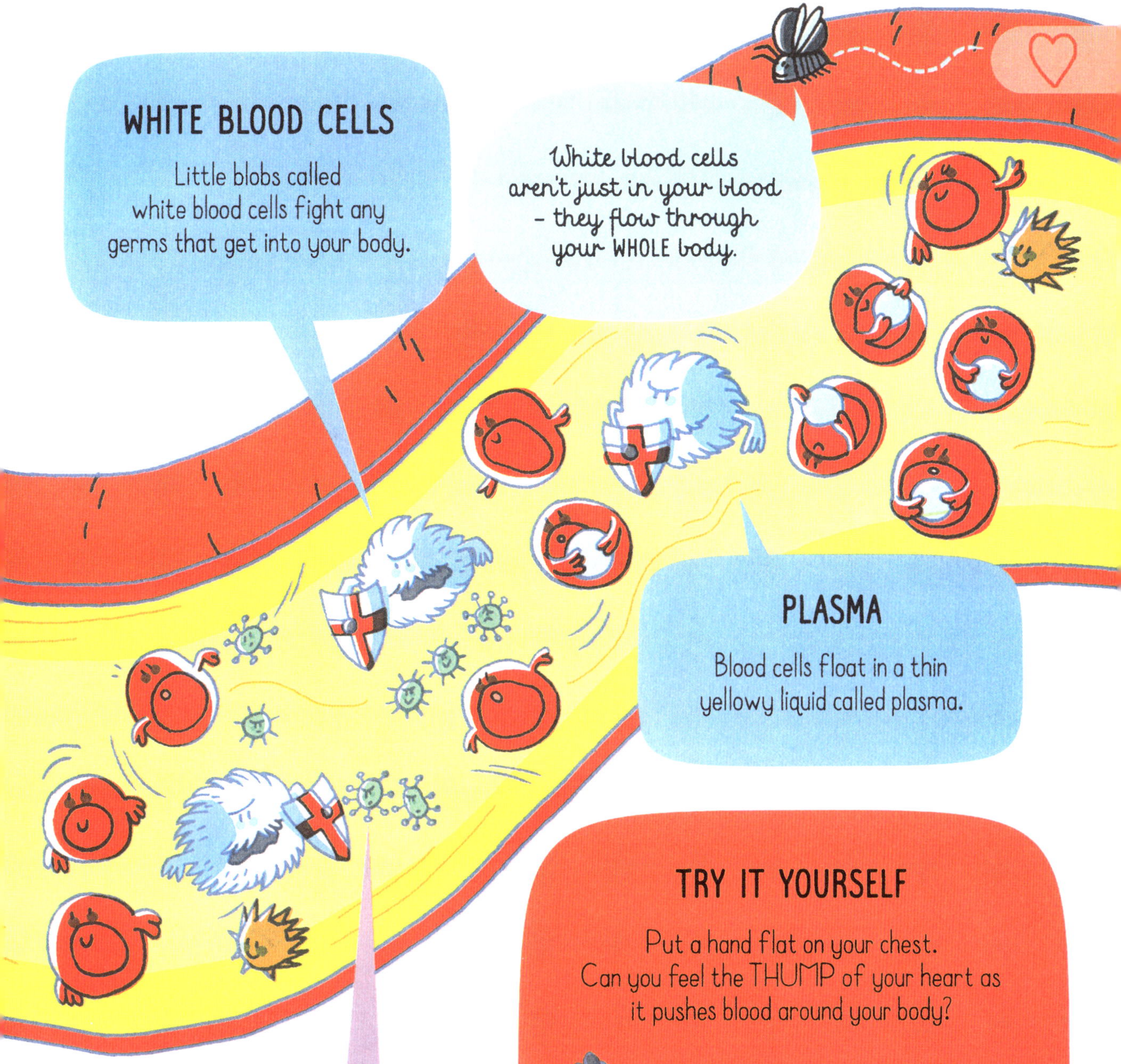

WHITE BLOOD CELLS

Little blobs called white blood cells fight any germs that get into your body.

White blood cells aren't just in your blood – they flow through your WHOLE body.

PLASMA

Blood cells float in a thin yellowy liquid called plasma.

GERMS

Germs aren't part of your blood, but they can travel in your blood. Here, white blood cells are fighting them.

TRY IT YOURSELF

Put a hand flat on your chest. Can you feel the THUMP of your heart as it pushes blood around your body?

Run up and down for a minute. Then feel your heart again.

The THUMP THUMP will be faster now. Your heart is pumping more quickly because your muscles need more blood when you exercise.

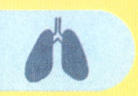

Breathe

The oxygen in your blood comes from the air all around you.
You get it from breathing – using your LUNGS.

Your lungs are two big spongy organs inside your chest.

When you breathe in, they fill with air. This is called INHALING.

When you breathe out, they empty again. This is called EXHALING.

LUNGS

WINDPIPE
Your windpipe connects your mouth and nose with your lungs.

DIAPHRAGM
Your diaphragm (say "die-a-fram") is a sheet of muscle. It moves up and down to help you breathe.

TRY IT YOURSELF

Put your hand on your chest and take a big breath in.

Can you feel your chest rise?

That's your lungs filling with air.

Sometimes your diaphragm jerks – and you get HICCUPS!

HIC!

Here's how your lungs work to get oxygen into your body.

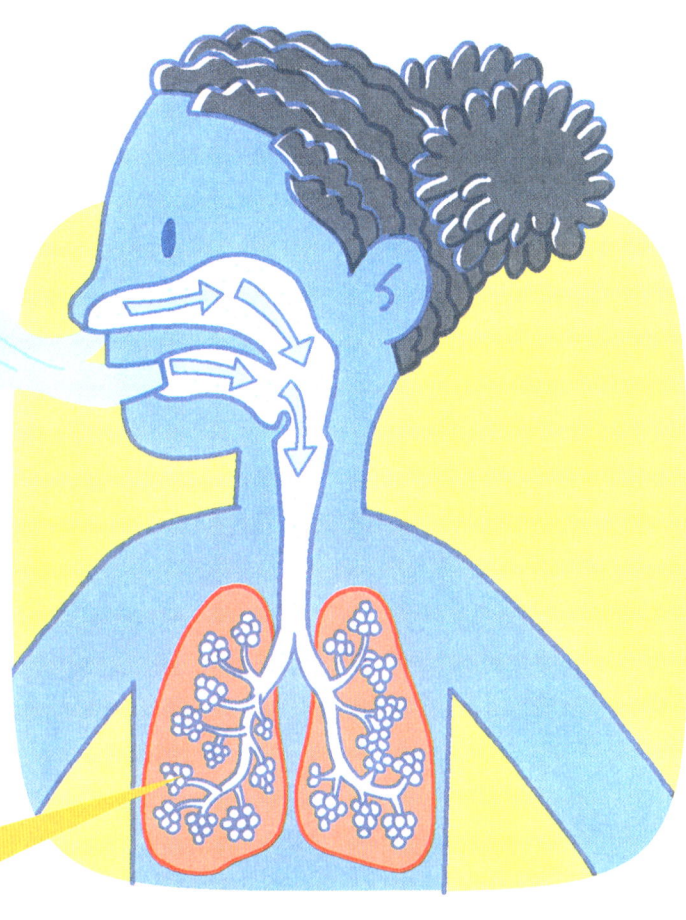

1. As you breathe in, air travels down your windpipe and into your lungs.

2. The air flows down smaller and smaller tubes, all through your lungs...

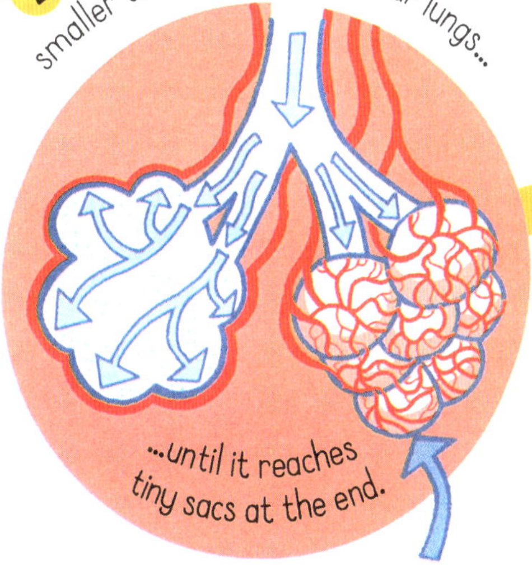

...until it reaches tiny sacs at the end.

3. Blood flows around the sac and collects the oxygen from the air.

Some people have a condition called asthma, which makes the tubes carrying air narrower.

Asthma can make it hard to breathe. But using an inhaler can help.

Munch, gurgle, plop!

Your body needs a range of foods and water every day.
When you eat, your DIGESTIVE SYSTEM gets to work.

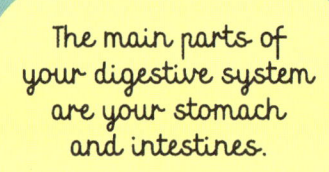

"The main parts of your digestive system are your stomach and intestines."

Your digestive system takes out good, useful things called NUTRIENTS from food.

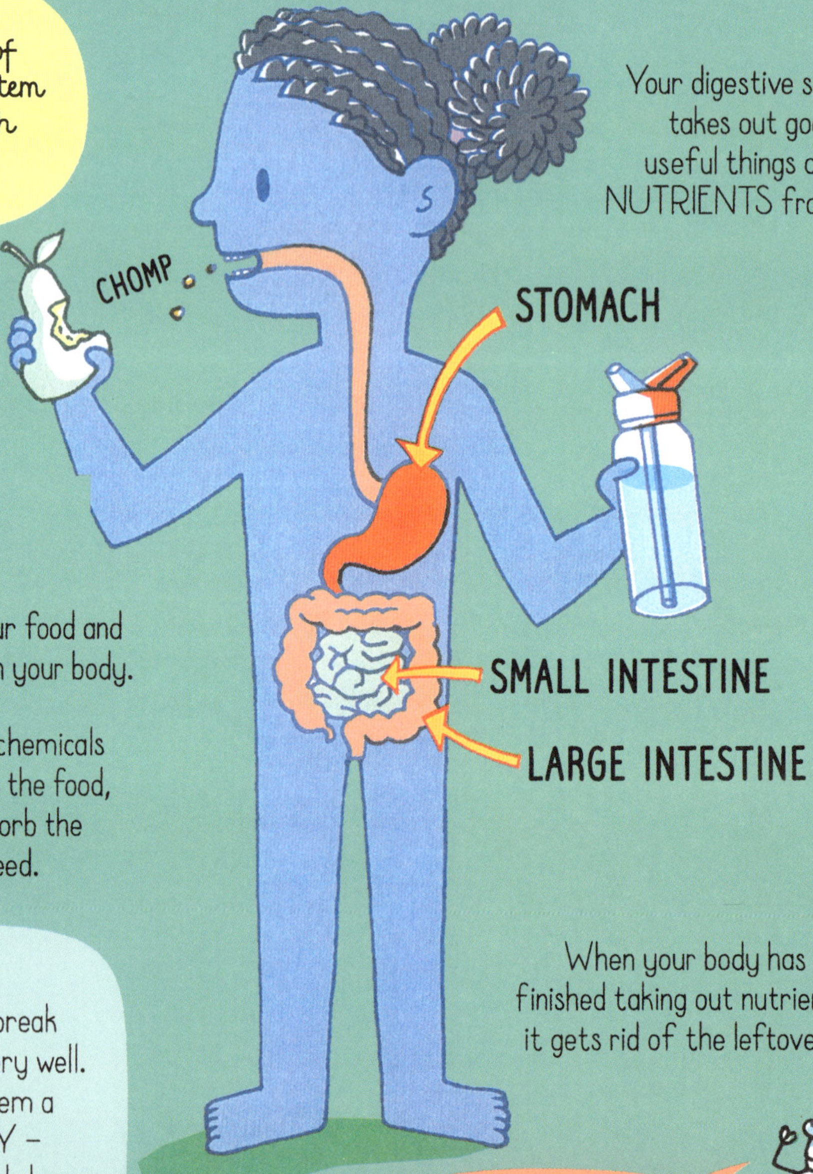

STOMACH

SMALL INTESTINE

LARGE INTESTINE

Muscles churn your food and squeeze it through your body.

Your body adds chemicals that break down the food, so you can absorb the bits you need.

When your body has finished taking out nutrients, it gets rid of the leftovers.

Some people can't break down certain foods very well. This might give them a FOOD ALLERGY – for example to milk and cheese.

"Usually, digesting food takes around THREE DAYS."

22

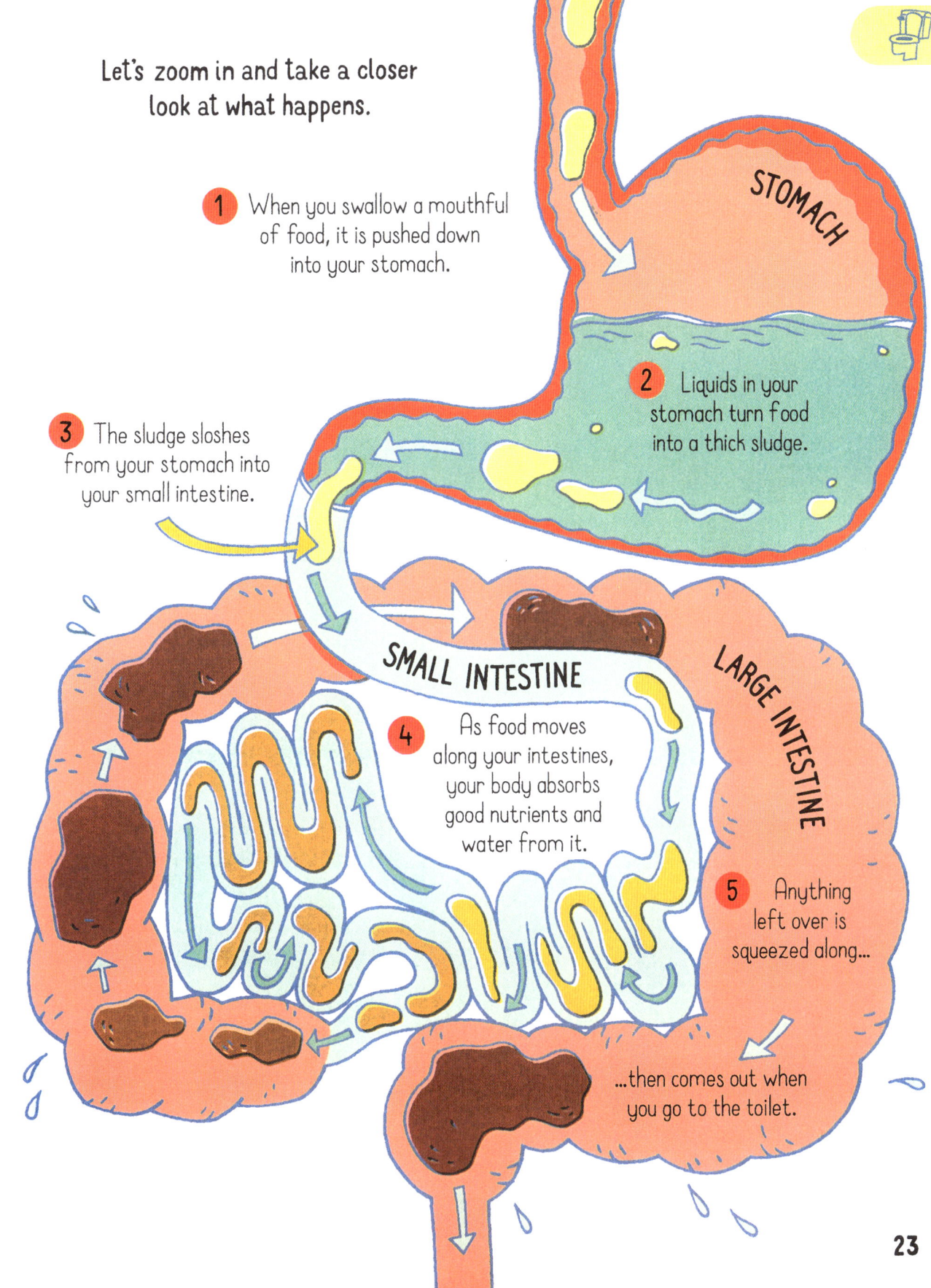

Your body also deals with what you drink – and gets rid of any extra water when you wee.

These are the organs that are in charge of making wee.

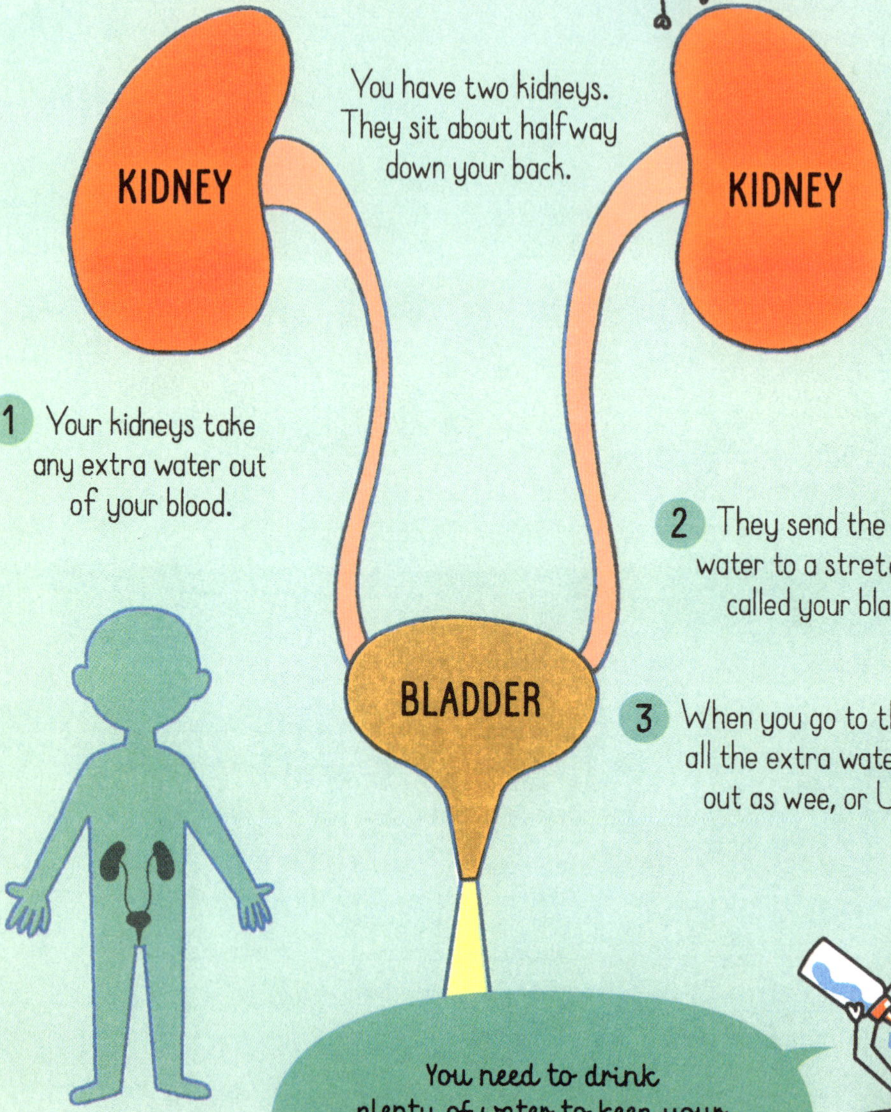

You have two kidneys. They sit about halfway down your back.

KIDNEY

KIDNEY

1. Your kidneys take any extra water out of your blood.

2. They send the extra water to a stretchy bag called your bladder.

BLADDER

3. When you go to the toilet, all the extra water comes out as wee, or URINE.

You need to drink plenty of water to keep your body running smoothly. There's more about it on page 47.

24

Eating and drinking also involves these other organs...

LIVER

Your liver is like a big chemical factory.

It has over 500 jobs, including helping to break down your food and removing any nasty parts.

An adult's liver is about as big as a rugby ball.

APPENDIX

Your appendix is a little curved organ attached to your intestine. Doctors aren't sure what it does.

Your appendix looks like this – and it's THIS BIG in real life.

Sometimes an appendix can swell up and become very painful. This is called APPENDICITIS. It can be cured by removing the appendix.

PANCREAS

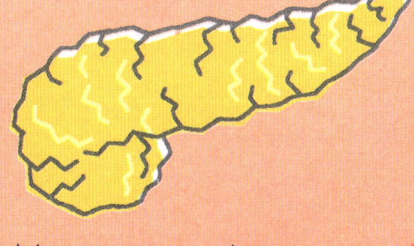

Your pancreas makes something called INSULIN, which controls how much sugar your blood can carry.

Some people have a condition called DIABETES. This means their pancreas doesn't work properly, so they might need insulin injections.

Your bones

Under your muscles you have a SKELETON made of hard BONES. Your skeleton supports your body – you'd be a wobbly lump without it.

Your skull is like a helmet protecting your brain.

Your LONGEST and STRONGEST bone is in your thigh.

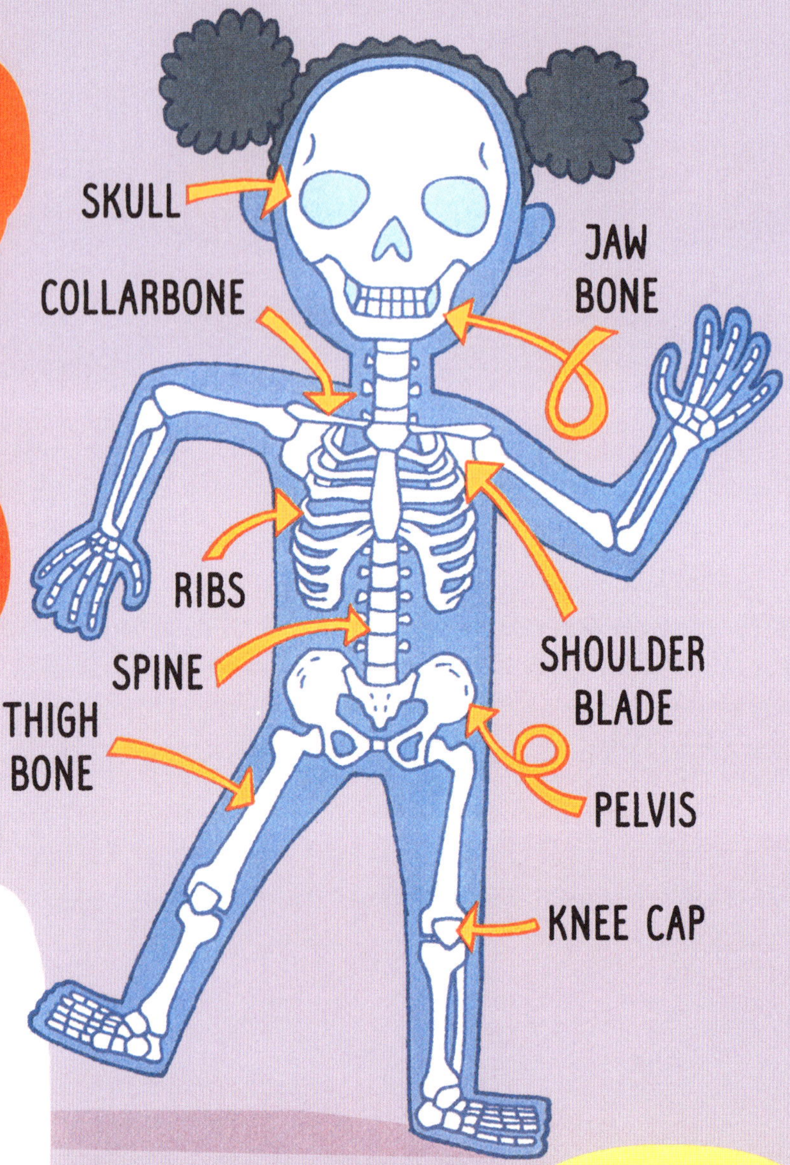

- SKULL
- JAW BONE
- COLLARBONE
- RIBS
- SPINE
- THIGH BONE
- SHOULDER BLADE
- PELVIS
- KNEE CAP

TRY IT YOURSELF

Gently poke different bits of your body.

If it's solid, you're feeling a bone. If it's squashy, you're feeling muscle and fat.

Babies have over 300 bones, but grown-ups have around 200.

That's because some bones join together as you grow up.

Your bones attach together at JOINTS.
Joints allow you to move around smoothly and easily.

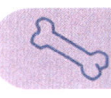

This joint can only bend up or down.
It's called a HINGE joint.

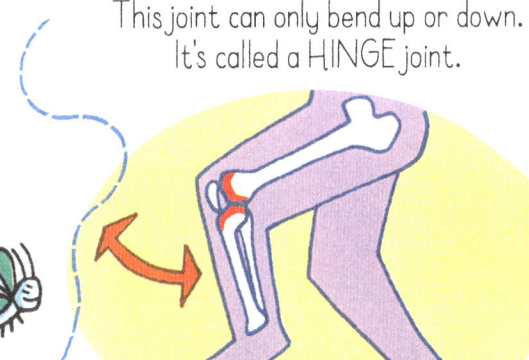

This joint can move in almost all directions.
It's called a BALL AND SOCKET joint.

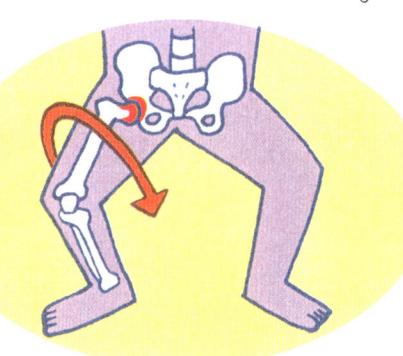

TRY IT YOURSELF

Move your knees and elbows. Can you feel how they move only up and down?
Now swing your whole arms around. The ball and socket joint in your
shoulder can move in almost all directions.

Your bones don't just hold you up and let you move.
They're also amazing blood-making machines.

Some bones have a soft,
spongy middle.
This is where some of
your blood is made.

It's called
BONE MARROW.

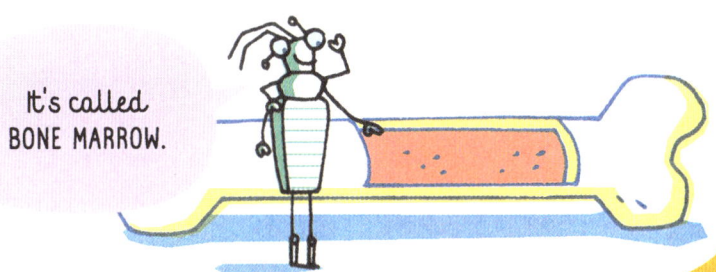

Busy brain

Inside your head is your BRAIN. It is a pale, squashy and wrinkled blob, that controls EVERYTHING you do.

> Your brain is in charge of your movements, from talking to walking.

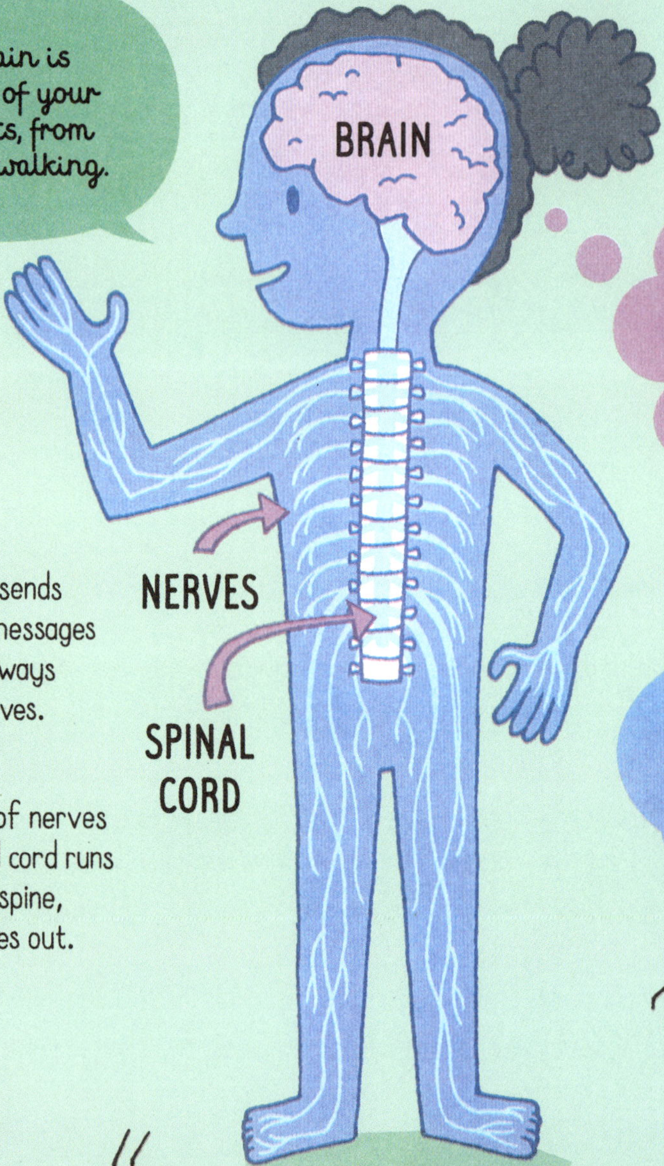

BRAIN

> Your brain is also where your thoughts happen.

Your brain sends and receives messages along pathways called nerves.

A thick bundle of nerves called the spinal cord runs down your spine, then branches out.

NERVES

SPINAL CORD

> Messages come to your brain from your senses.

You can read about how your senses work from page 32.

Your brain is divided up into sections. Each section has its own jobs. Here are just SOME of the things the different sections do.

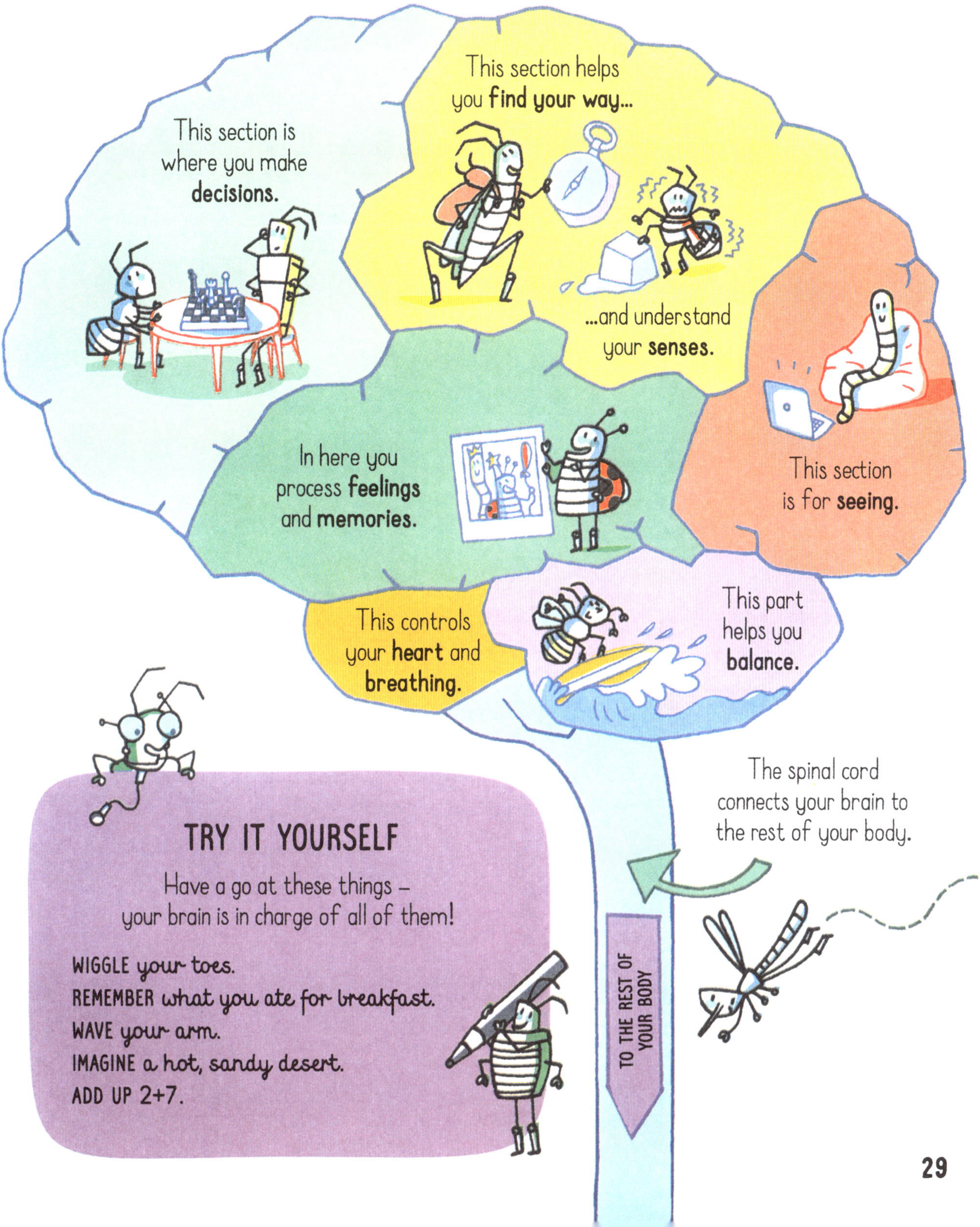

This section is where you make **decisions**.

This section helps you **find your way**...

...and understand your **senses**.

In here you process **feelings** and **memories**.

This section is for **seeing**.

This controls your **heart** and **breathing**.

This part helps you **balance**.

The spinal cord connects your brain to the rest of your body.

TO THE REST OF YOUR BODY

TRY IT YOURSELF

Have a go at these things – your brain is in charge of all of them!

WIGGLE your toes.
REMEMBER what you ate for breakfast.
WAVE your arm.
IMAGINE a hot, sandy desert.
ADD UP 2+7.

Your brain makes and stores your thoughts, dreams and memories.

THOUGHTS

All the time you're awake, your brain is busy thinking.
You need to think about most things you do.

Chatting   Reading   Learning   Playing

IMAGINATION

Your imagination lets your brain make things up.

What about a bike that could go up walls?

ZOOM

What if plants could talk?

There's a caterpillar tickling me heeheee.

I wonder what I will do when I grow up?

DREAMS

Dreams happen when you're asleep.
They're usually a mix of things from real life and your imagination.

Bad dreams are called nightmares.
They can be scary – but they're not real.

MEMORIES

Memories are moments from your life, stored in your brain.

Some memories last
a couple of seconds.
Others can last years.

When you sleep,
your brain sorts through your
memories of the day and
decides which ones to keep.

Your senses

Every day, your SENSES are taking in messages from the outside world, and sending them to your brain.

TASTE
Your mouth and tongue let you taste things.

SPICY SOUR SWEET

Yum!

SMELL
Your nose lets you smell things.

FLOWERY FRESH ROTTEN

Taste and smell can help you avoid foods that might make you sick.

TOUCH
Touch tells you about the texture and temperature of things. It also keeps you safe by telling you when something HURTS.

SPIKY SMOOTH COLD HOT

32

Have a go at testing your own senses.

Test your taste

Take a small cube of apple and a small cube of raw carrot.

Close your eyes, and pinch your nose so you can't smell anything.

Ask someone to pass you one cube at a time and eat it.

Can you tell which is which?

You probably won't be able to. Without your sense of smell, your sense of taste doesn't work as well.

Test your touch

Ask someone in your house to find a few safe objects with a similar shape, and put them in a bag.

Shut your eyes tight. Feel the objects one by one.

Can you work out what they are?

You'll need to pay extra attention to the SHAPES and TEXTURES.

Sometimes people have a sense that doesn't work, so they have other ways to manage.

Some people can't hear very well, or hear at all. Not being able to hear is called being deaf.

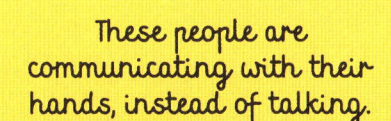

These people are communicating with their hands, instead of talking.

It's called SIGN LANGUAGE.

This sign means "please" in American Sign Language.

This sign means "thank you" in British Sign Language.

Some people can't see very well, or see at all. Not being able to see is called being blind.

This is my assistance dog. She acts like my eyes and keeps me safe.

I use this cane to help me find my way.

Let's take a closer look at **how your eyes and ears work.**

Under your eyelids, your eye is a round ball. This is what it looks like up close.

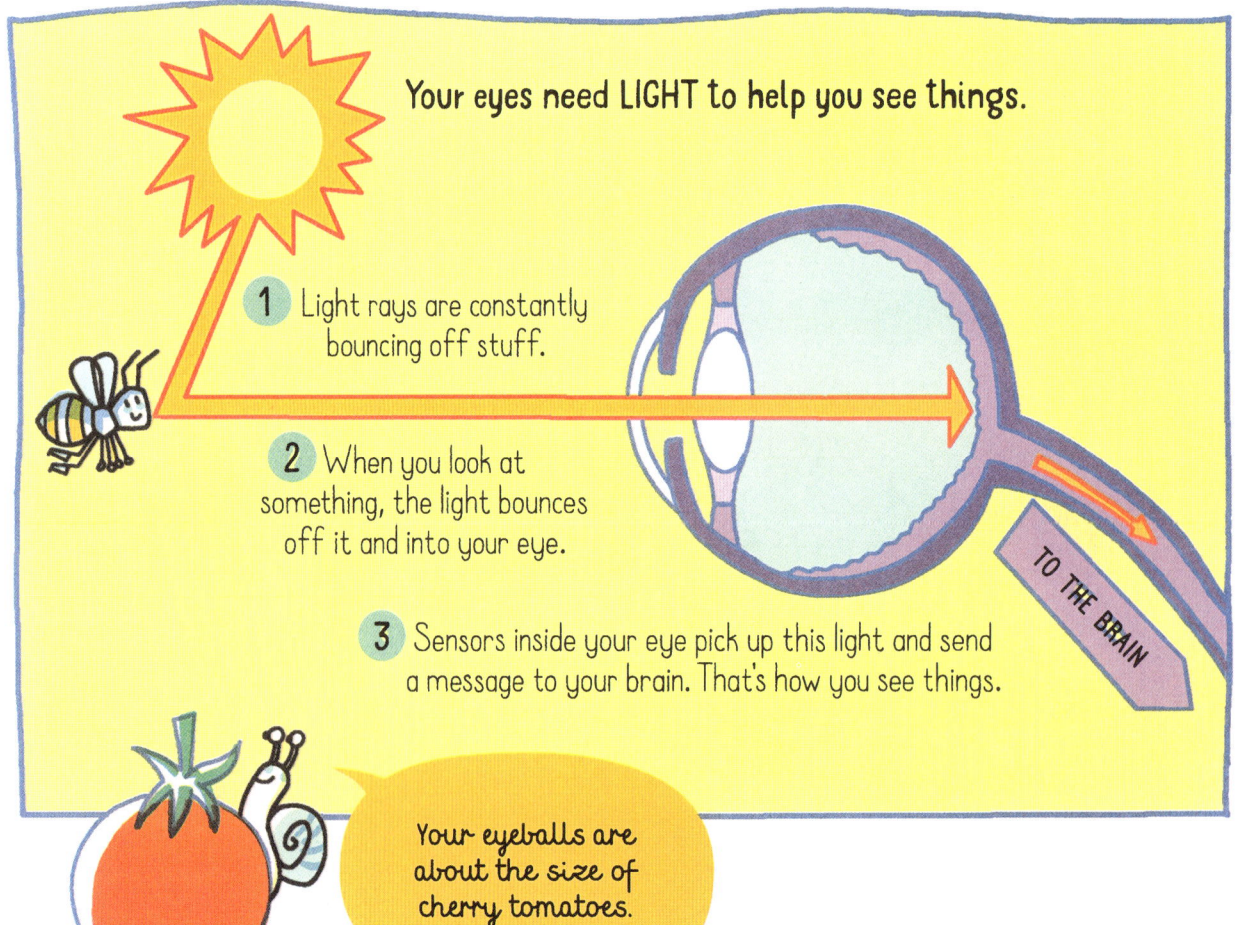

The coloured circle is called the IRIS.

The black dot is called the PUPIL. It's a hole that lets light into your eyes.

What colour are your eyes?

When it's dark, your pupils get BIGGER, to let in more light.

Your eyes need LIGHT to help you see things.

1. Light rays are constantly bouncing off stuff.

2. When you look at something, the light bounces off it and into your eye.

TO THE BRAIN

3. Sensors inside your eye pick up this light and send a message to your brain. That's how you see things.

Your eyeballs are about the size of cherry tomatoes.

Any time something makes a sound,
it causes movements, or vibrations, in the air.

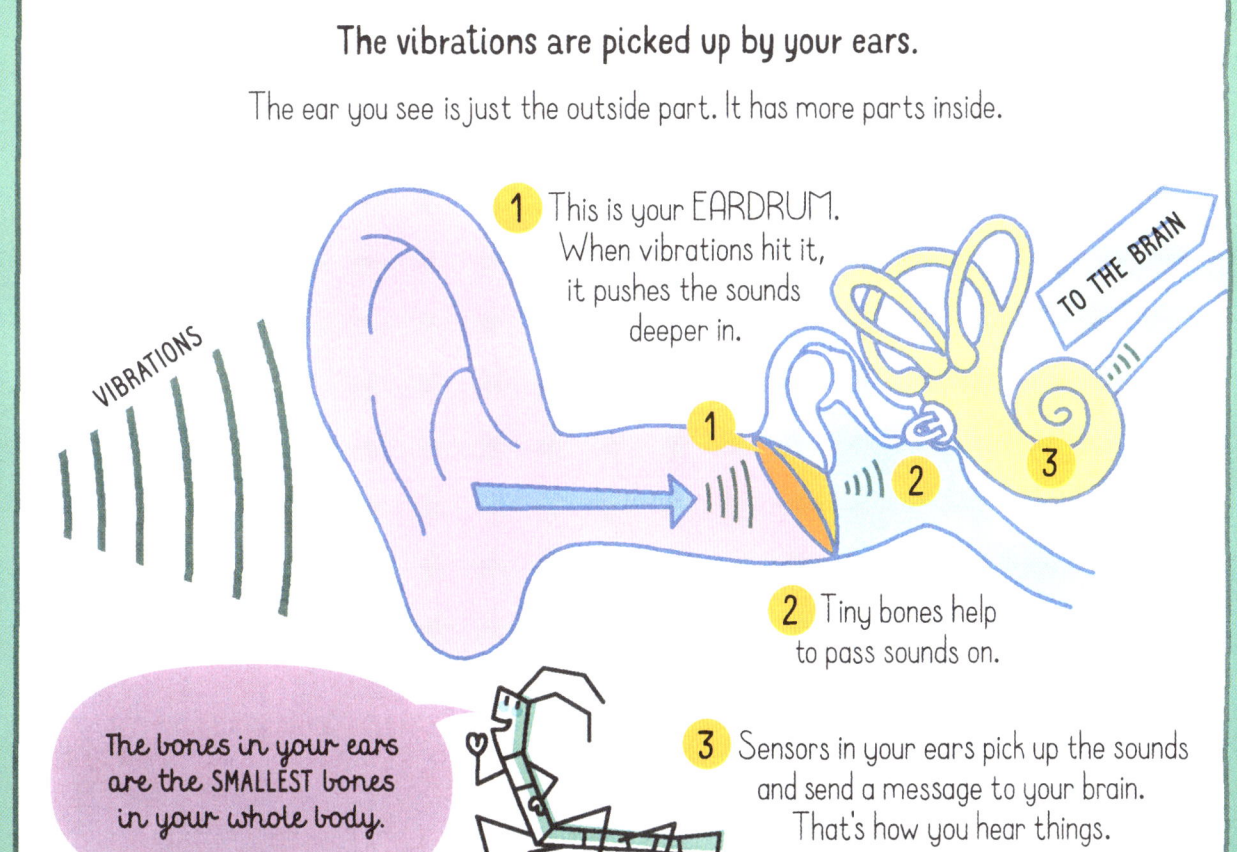

THUMP CLAP TSSSS BANG DING!

The Beetles

The vibrations are picked up by your ears.

The ear you see is just the outside part. It has more parts inside.

VIBRATIONS

1 This is your EARDRUM. When vibrations hit it, it pushes the sounds deeper in.

TO THE BRAIN

2 Tiny bones help to pass sounds on.

The bones in your ears are the SMALLEST bones in your whole body.

3 Sensors in your ears pick up the sounds and send a message to your brain. That's how you hear things.

37

Lots of feelings

How are you feeling right now?
Feelings, or EMOTIONS, are a big part of being a person.

Emotions often show on your face.
Here's what some of the main emotions can look like.

You might hear an emotion in someone's voice, too.

SCARED

ARGH!

HAPPY

How many of these emotions do you recognise?

EXCITED

Wow!

SAD

Waaah.

GRUMPY

Hmph.

PLEASED

You might feel all of these emotions in a day.
Or you might not really notice any strong emotions at all.

NERVOUS

Err...

CALM

GRR!

ANGRY

EMBARRASSED

CONFUSED

Huh?

SILLY

DISGUSTED

Eewwww.

SHOCKED

I'm HUNGRY. Is that an emotion?

No but it can AFFECT your emotions. If you don't eat, it can make you feel grumpy.

How you feel can show in your whole body.

Fidgety legs or hands can mean "I feel worried."

Shrugging shoulders can mean "I don't know."

Looking down with arms crossed can mean "I feel sad."

Sending signals with your body is called BODY LANGUAGE. It can help you communicate, even with people who don't speak the same language.

Hola!

Konnichiwa!

Bonjour!

A friendly wave means HELLO all over the world.

Spain

Japan

France

Body language can also help you to understand someone who can't speak at all.

Rubbing eyes probably means this baby is sleepy.

Uh oh, crying! I think this baby is hungry or uncomfortable.

Look at the body language in these pictures. How do you think each of these people is feeling?

1

2

3

A — HOORAY! I'm having a great day!

B — I'm telling you off.

C — I'm so UPSET.

Answers: 1.B, 2.C, 3.A

Emotions can change the way your whole body feels.
Some emotions feel nice.
Others can be unpleasant or overwhelming.

When you are HAPPY, your brain releases super-duper feel-good chemicals. The chemicals make your whole body feel calm and relaxed.

What a great birthday! I feel so happy!

TOOT

When you feel SAD or upset, you might cry. That's just your body dealing with the feeling.

Waaaah.

42

When you are ANGRY, your heart beats fast and you can feel hot and flustered.

Oh no! Your lovely tower!

THUMP

POP!

When you are FRIGHTENED, your heart beats more quickly. You might freeze up or run away.

ARGH! Too loud.

When you hug someone you love, your brain can send messages to your body that make you feel CALM.

43

Here are some tips to help you get through more difficult emotions.

IF YOU FEEL ANGRY...

...cool down. If you feel hot, you could open a window, or take your jumper off.

Cooling your body down can cool down the angry feeling too.

1...2...3...4...

...count to 10. This helps your body slow down and feel calmer.

With any difficult emotion, talking to someone you trust can help.

Sharing your feelings can make them seem less scary and big.

IF YOU FEEL SAD...

...do something you enjoy to cheer yourself up.

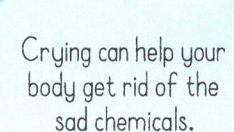

...have a little cry.

Crying can help your body get rid of the sad chemicals.

IF YOU FEEL WORRIED...

...listen to some music you like, or a story.

...take big, slow, deep breaths. Like counting, this can help to calm you down.

Listening to music or a story can push any noisy thoughts out of your head.

Staying healthy

Your body is a complicated machine.
It needs lots of things to keep it running smoothly.

Food gives you energy, and the substances you need to grow and make repairs.

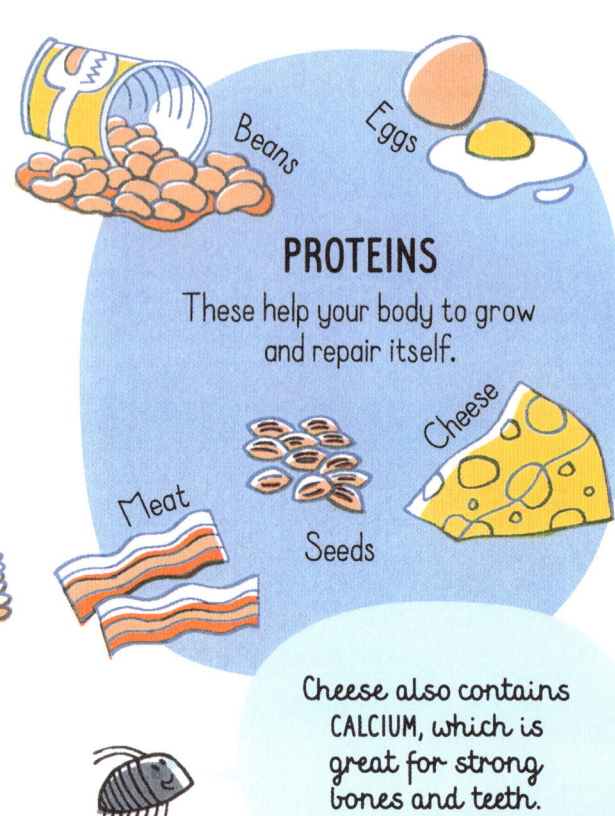

Bread

Rice

CARBOHYDRATES
These give you long-lasting energy.

Pasta

Potatoes

Noodles

Beans

Eggs

PROTEINS
These help your body to grow and repair itself.

Meat

Seeds

Cheese

Cheese also contains CALCIUM, which is great for strong bones and teeth.

Sugary snacks give you energy too, but it wears off quickly.

FATS
You need a small amount of fat to keep your hair and skin healthy.

Avocados

Nuts

Olive oil

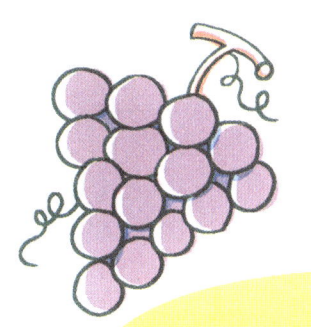

FRUIT AND VEG

Fruits and vegetables contain super substances called VITAMINS, that keep you healthy.

You need to eat a range of fruits and vegetables to get ALL your vitamins.

Citrus fruits (including oranges and lemons) are packed with VITAMIN C. This helps your body to fight illnesses.

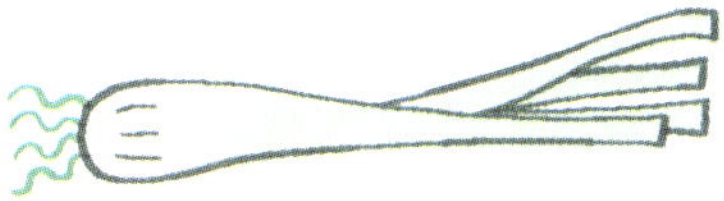

Carrots help you to make VITAMIN A, which is good for your eyesight.

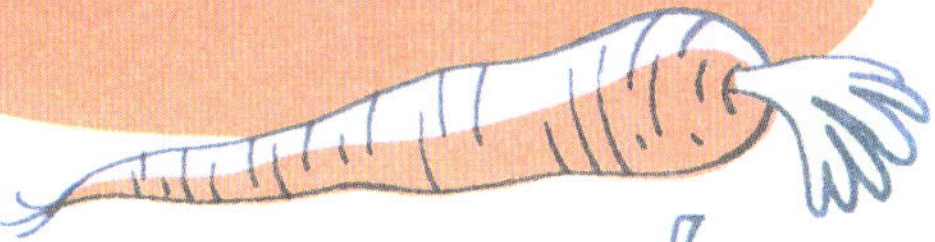

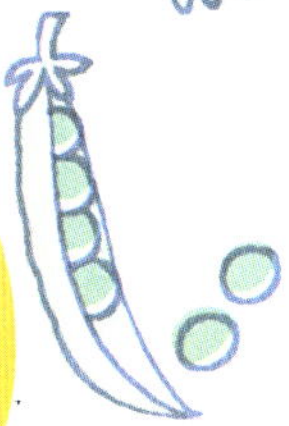

Broccoli and other green vegetables contain VITAMIN K. This helps your body to heal cuts.

Fruit and veg also contain FIBRE, which helps your digestive system to work smoothly.

WATER

Water is very important for staying healthy. It keeps your whole body working properly.

Your body needs 5-6 glasses of water each day – or more if it's hot!

Your body also needs EXERCISE. Exercise is good for...

STRONG BONES

Exercise makes your bones stronger and tougher, especially when you're growing.

STRONG HEART AND LUNGS

Exercise makes your heart and lungs work harder.

Heart

Lungs

You breathe faster when you exercise.

FLEXIBILITY

Being flexible means your body can move, bend and stretch.

FEELING GREAT

Doing exercise releases chemicals that make you feel happy.

Here are a few exercises you could do at home to get your body moving and your heart pumping.

Run on the spot

How fast can you move your feet?

Hold your body like a plank off the floor.

How long can you hold it?

Dance around

Star jumps

BOING

Punch the air

Crouch down low to the floor...

Frog jumps

...then spring up as high as you can!

49

Keeping CLEAN makes it harder for germs to get into your body and make you ill.

Have a shower or a bath when you need it.

There's more about germs on pages 52-53.

Cover your mouth and nose when you cough or sneeze.

ACHOO!

Clean and cover up cuts and scrapes.

Wash your hands, especially after going to the toilet and before eating.

Warm, soapy water kills germs.

Brush your teeth twice a day.

50

A good night's SLEEP lets your body make repairs, file away memories, and build up energy for tomorrow.

Here are some tips for having the BEST night's sleep you can.

Shut out bright light.

Go to bed around the same time each day.

A dark room tells your brain that it's time to sleep.

Unwind before bed by reading or listening to a story.

If you don't like the dark, you could put a night light on.

Don't worry if you take a while to drift off, or wake up in the night.

Just lying in bed is still a good rest.

Being ill

GERMS are tiny things that can make you ill if they get inside you. Different germs cause different illnesses.

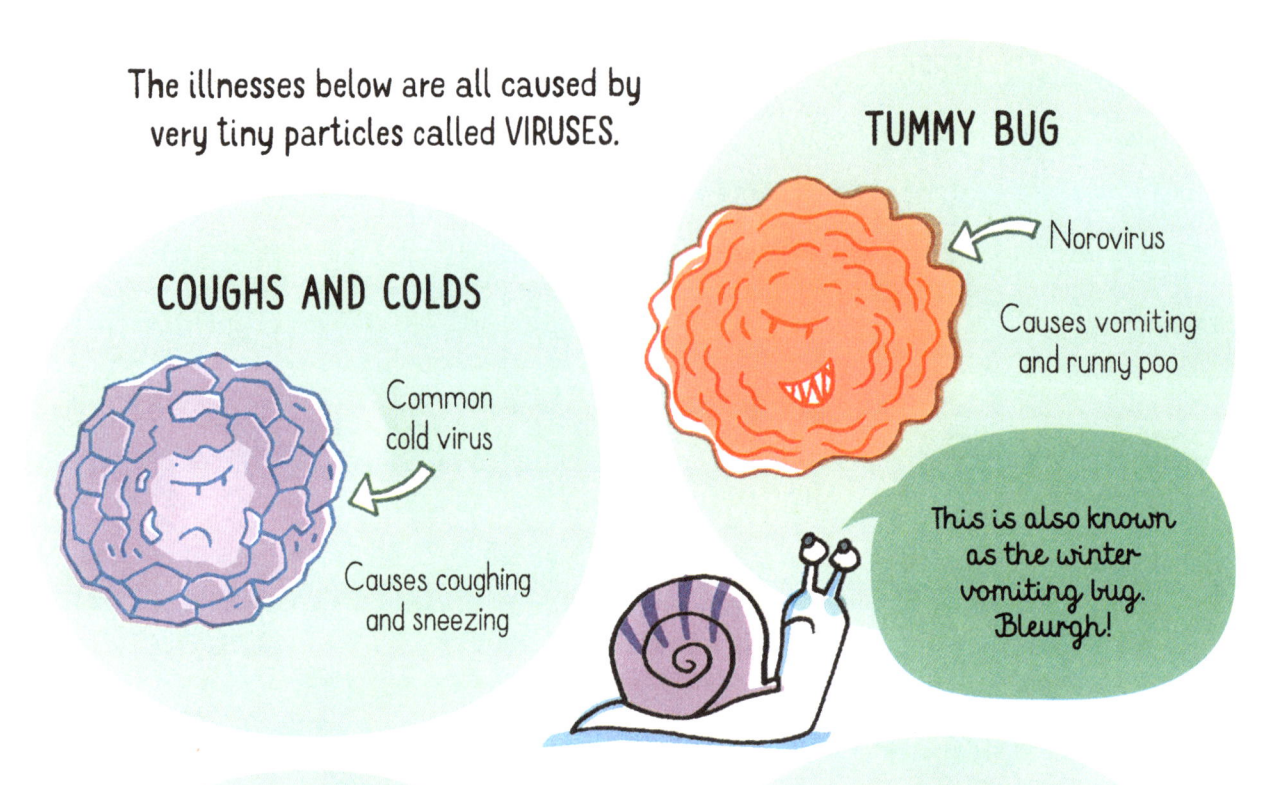

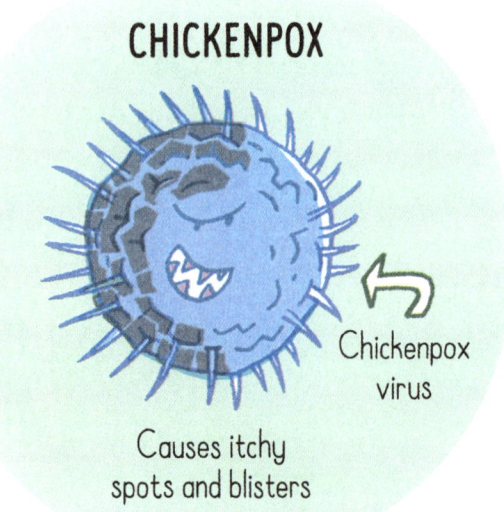

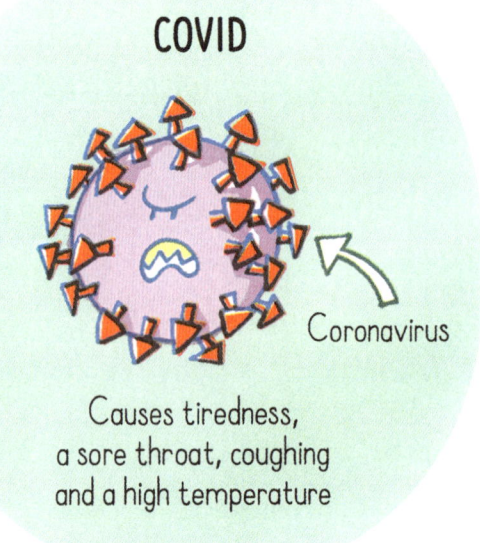

The illnesses below are all caused by very tiny particles called VIRUSES.

COUGHS AND COLDS

Common cold virus

Causes coughing and sneezing

TUMMY BUG

Norovirus

Causes vomiting and runny poo

This is also known as the winter vomiting bug. Bleurgh!

CHICKENPOX

Chickenpox virus

Causes itchy spots and blisters

COVID

Coronavirus

Causes tiredness, a sore throat, coughing and a high temperature

Other illnesses are caused by tiny living things called BACTERIA (although most bacteria are harmless).

FOOD POISONING

E. coli bacteria

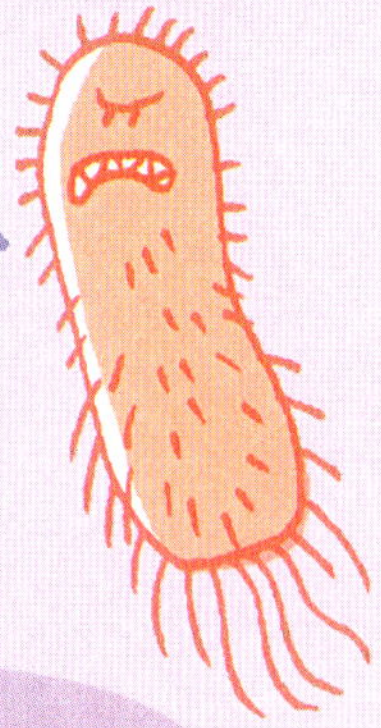

Causes vomiting, tummy ache and runny poo

EAR INFECTION

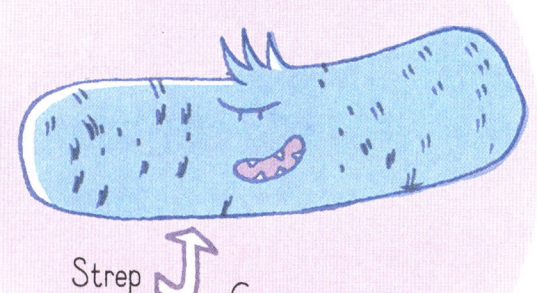

Strep bacteria

Causes sore ears and dizziness

Hand-washing and cooking food properly are the best ways to avoid food poisoning.

Sometimes very small living creatures can live on your body too.

HEADLICE

These little bugs can live in hair and give you itchy bites.

WORMS

These little worms can give you an itchy bottom.

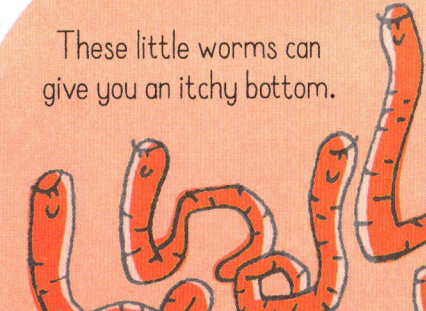

Special combs and shampoos can get rid of lice, and medicines can sort out worms.

What happens in your body when you're ill?

You might feel hot and sweaty, or cold and shivery. That's called having a fever.

Your body is fighting the infection by making it too hot for germs to survive.

Coughs and sneezes help to push germs out of your body.

ACHOO!

GURGLE

Being sick empties your tummy to get rid of germs.

While you're ill there's a big fight going on inside your body.

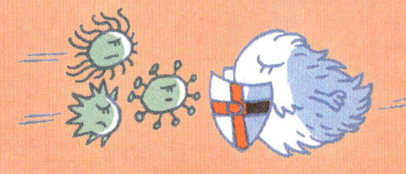

Your blood is flooded with white blood cells that fight germs. It can make you feel really tired.

Beetle's guide to Getting Better

You can get better from most common illnesses in a few days. Here are some of the things that can help your body get better.

Drink lots of water and other drinks. Liquids help your body flush out germs.

Get lots of rest! Your body needs to use all your energy for getting better.

Medicines can lower your temperature and stop any aches or pains.

If you have a sore throat, drinking warm water with lemon and honey can help.

Sometimes you might need to see a doctor. Doctors can give you medicines to help fight the bugs.

Sometimes you might get bumps, scrapes, bites and stings. Looking after them is called FIRST AID.

CUTS AND GRAZES

If you break your skin, it bleeds. Bleeding helps to clean the cut. When the blood dries, it forms a scab which protects the cut while it gets better.

This is a bottle of ANTISEPTIC, which kills germs. You can spray it onto a cut to make it clean.

I fell over!

These are DRESSINGS. They go over a clean cut, so germs can't get inside.

BUMPS AND BRUISES

If something hits you and breaks a blood vessel under your skin, you get a BRUISE. Bruises can swell up into bumps too.

ICE

An ice pack can help bumps and sore body parts feel better.

BITES AND STINGS

Bites and stings from insects and spiky plants can feel very sore or itchy.

If you have a sting or thorn stuck in your skin, you can try to pull it out.

Bite and sting cream can help to soothe an itchy bite or rash.

If a bite is sore, an ice cube against it can stop it from hurting.

BURNS

If you touch something hot, you may get a burn.

You should run a burn under lots of cold water, to cool it down.

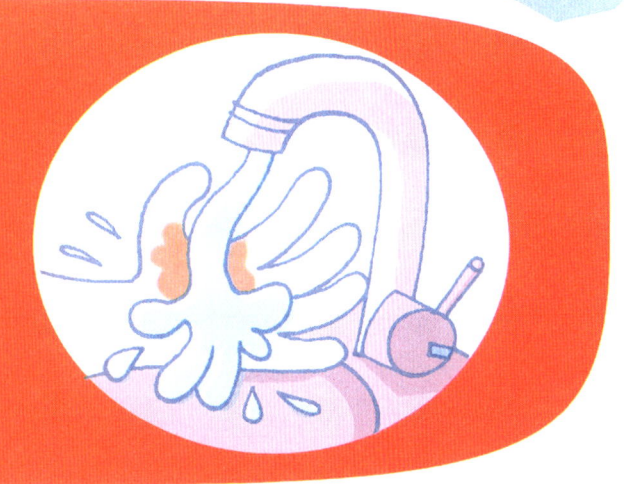

You can treat little injuries at home.

For bigger injuries you might need to go to a hospital. Turn the page to find out more.

Take a look inside a **hospital**. People with different problems are all being seen to and helped.

CHECK-UPS

These people are waiting for appointments.

- I'm getting the dressing on my leg changed.
- I'm having a scan of the baby growing in my tummy.
- I'm having some blood taken for tests.

ACCIDENT AND EMERGENCY

This is where people come when they need to be seen quickly. It's very busy.

- I've got a strange pain in my chest — can you find out what's wrong?
- You hit your head. We're checking that you're OK.
- That's a bad cut. We'll need to stitch it up.

X-RAYS

An X-ray is a photo that shows what's happening under your skin.

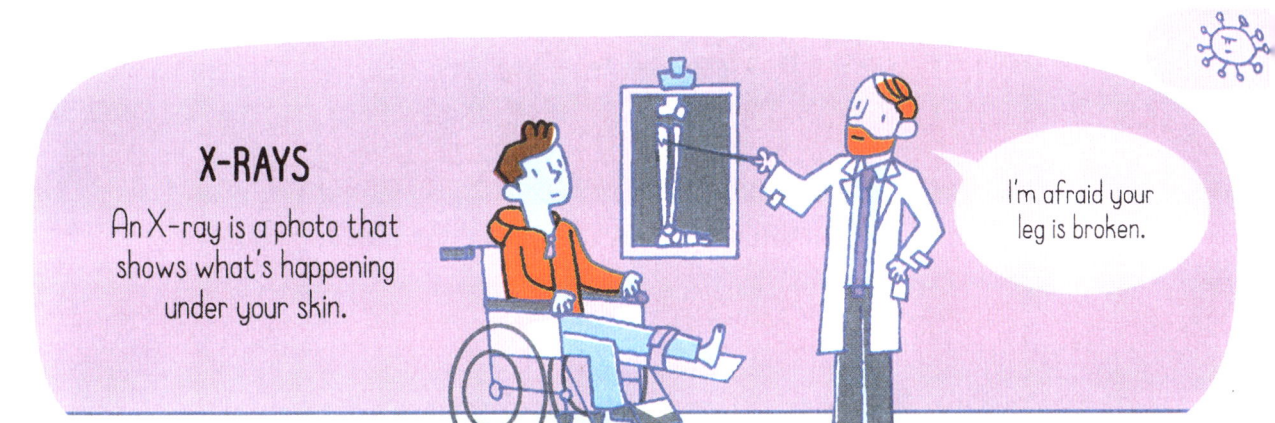

I'm afraid your leg is broken.

OPERATIONS

Doctors called surgeons can look inside people's bodies and fix things.

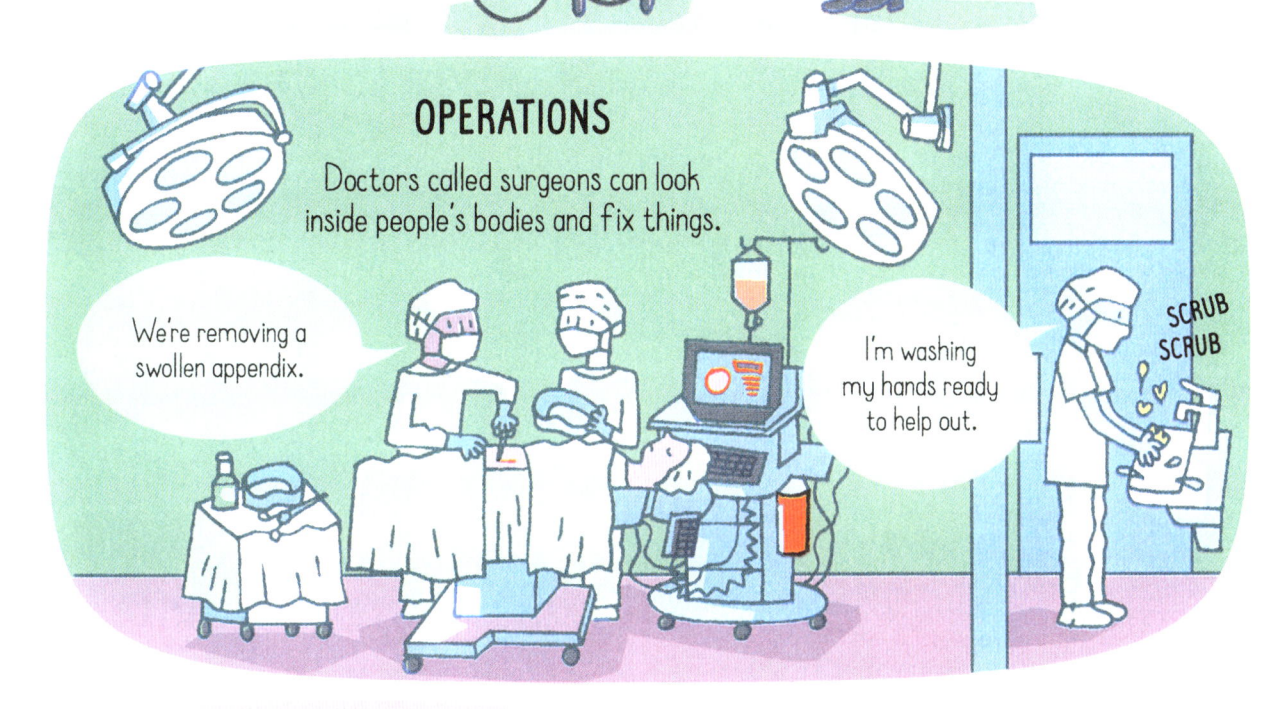

We're removing a swollen appendix.

I'm washing my hands ready to help out.

SCRUB SCRUB

NEW BABIES

This tiny baby has just been born.

WAHHHHHH WAHHHHHH

TIME TO TALK

I help people to talk through difficult feelings.

Allergies

Lots of people find that something – such as a type of food – makes them SNEEZY or ITCHY or UNWELL. Doctors call this having an ALLERGY.

I'm allergic to pollen – the yellowy powder made by plants. It makes me very sneezy.

ACHOO! ACHOO!

Being allergic to pollen is called HAYFEVER.

Hayfever is the most common allergy in the world.

When you have an allergy, your body reacts to something that's normally harmless.

Reactions might be a runny nose, a red rash or lots of sneezes.

These are my anti-allergy tablets.

Luckily, medicines can help to calm the reaction.

Some people are very allergic to one type of food. Accidentally eating or even just touching it could make them dangerously ill. So they carry medicine with them all the time.

I'm allergic to nuts. I keep my anti-allergy medicine in my backpack.

I have an allergy to dust. It makes my eyes itch. So I try to keep things dust-free.

VROOM

If I eat eggs, I get a rash. So I always check ingredients, to make sure I don't eat eggs by accident.

An egg allergy is one of the most common allergies in children. But most children grow out of it as they get older.

Do you know anyone with allergies?

Growing and changing

Your body is always changing – sometimes slowly and sometimes quickly. Here's what one person's life might look like.

BEFORE BEING BORN

Everyone starts off as a teeny blob...

...that gets bigger...

...and starts to look like a baby.

7-12 YEARS OLD

Look at me go!

Children do lots of growing, moving, learning and playing.

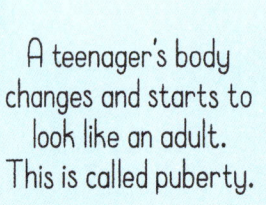

4-6 YEARS OLD

I'm off to learn!

Time to start school...

13-17 YEARS OLD

Teenager

A teenager's body changes and starts to look like an adult. This is called puberty.

18 AND UP

In different countries, you officially become an adult at different ages.

Adult

Everyone grows and changes at different rates — this is just a rough guide.

How old are you? Where are you on the timeline below?

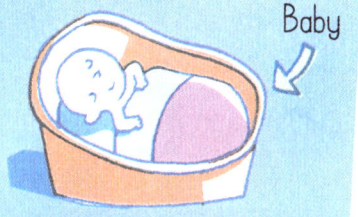

JUST BORN

Baby

Most babies are born after about 9 months.

0-1 YEAR OLD

Newborn babies grow and change really quickly.

1-3 YEARS OLD

Toddler

Blab blerb.

As toddlers get older they can do more and more.

HAPPY RETIREMENT

Most adults work until they're around 60-70, then stop working to have more time to relax.

70 AND OLDER

Eventually, people's lives and bodies slow down.

In your first years, your body is growing REALLY quickly.
Every day brings changes.

When babies are born, they can't do much for themselves.
Over the next months and years, they have to learn to...

EAT

CRAWL

TALK

Cat.

STAND UP

WALK

Growing starts with your BONES.

Your bones grow at each end, making your body and arms and legs longer.

Sometimes your growth speeds up. This is called a growth spurt.

Oops!

Growth spurts can make you clumsy, while your brain gets used to how long your arms and legs are now.

As a teenager, your body and brain change EVEN more, as you become an adult. You might become...

SMARTER

You'll learn LOADS.

MORE INDEPENDENT

You can do more stuff on your own.

A DIFFERENT SHAPE

As well as getting taller, you might get more curves or bigger muscles.

You'll also sweat more...

...get hairier...

...and you might get spots.

These changes happen at different times for everyone, and take a few years.

65

When you finally get to be an adult, you can do new things.
For example, you might...

LIVE ON YOUR OWN

GET MARRIED

BUY A HOUSE

SOLD

DRIVE A CAR

START A FAMILY

LOOK AFTER YOUR OWN MONEY

VOTE

VOTE FOR WHO SHOULD BE IN CHARGE

You don't HAVE to do these things, but you can if you want to.

When I'm a grown-up, I'll eat ice cream for breakfast!

In old age, your body starts to slow down.
Some people need more help reading and getting around.

"I can't see as well as I used to."

"My stick helps me to balance."

"I use a frame for walking."

"I'm still jogging, byeeee."

"I've got a new phone with big numbers on so I can use it more easily."

"I can hear you much better with my new hearing aids."

Every life comes to an end at some point.

When someone dies, people who love them gather together to remember their life.

It can feel very sad when someone dies. Remembering them and sharing memories with others can help.

67

What makes you YOU

You are unique. There's no one exactly like you!
But you are probably SIMILAR to some people – especially people in your family.

Children often look similar to their parents.
That's because how they look has been PASSED ON.

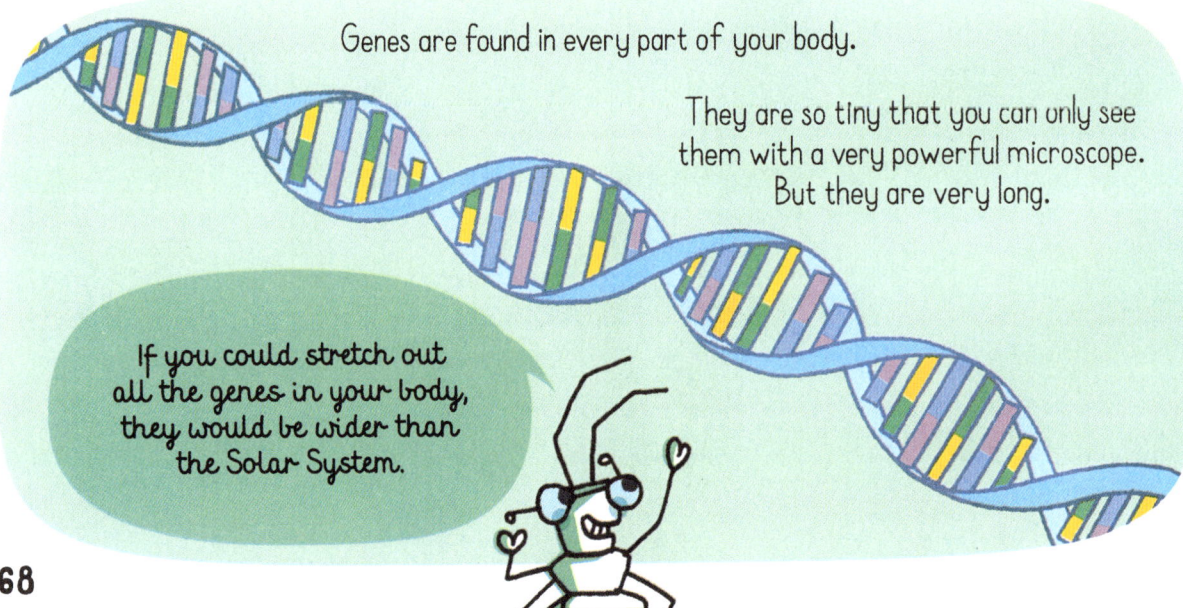

People always say I look like my dad!

Your body is shaped by tiny instructions called GENES – which are passed on from parents to children.

Genes control your eye colour, hair colour and even what kind of EARWAX you have!

Genes are found in every part of your body.

They are so tiny that you can only see them with a very powerful microscope. But they are very long.

If you could stretch out all the genes in your body, they would be wider than the Solar System.

**What you're like isn't ONLY about genes.
The way you live and the people around you make a difference, too.**

We all wear the same sorts of clothes.

We all like board games.

We play in the sea EVERY day!

Who you are is also about the choices you make.

I love learning languages.

J'aime apprendre les langues.

Me encanta aprender idiomas.

I dye my hair.

I lift lots of weights, so now I've got bigger muscles.

Amazing body facts

You have more than
600 MUSCLES
and
200 BONES
in your body.

Your brain contains over
80 BILLION NERVE CELLS.
Even a piece of brain the size of a speck of sand contains
100,000
of them.

Your sneezes can reach
160 KM/H (100 MPH).
That's faster than most cars!

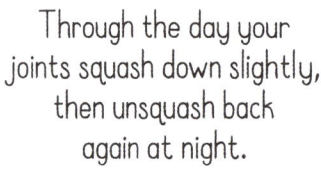

You are
1 CM TALLER
in the morning!
Through the day your joints squash down slightly, then unsquash back again at night.

ACHOOOOO

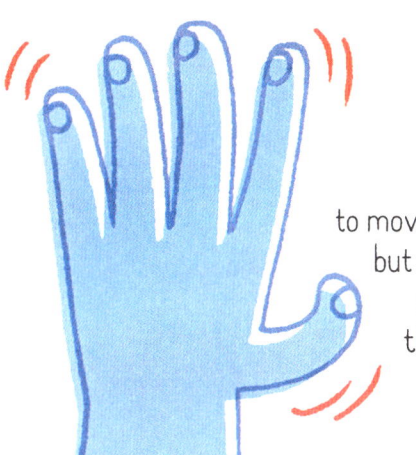

It takes
6
MUSCLES
to move each of your fingers... but those muscles aren't in your fingers – they're in your arm.

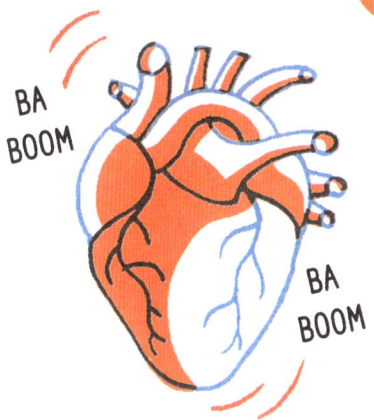

BA BOOM

BA BOOM

Your
HEART BEATS
100,000
times a day.
It's made of muscle that never ever gets tired.

Your smallest bone is smaller than
A GRAIN OF RICE.
It's one of the tiny bones in your ear.

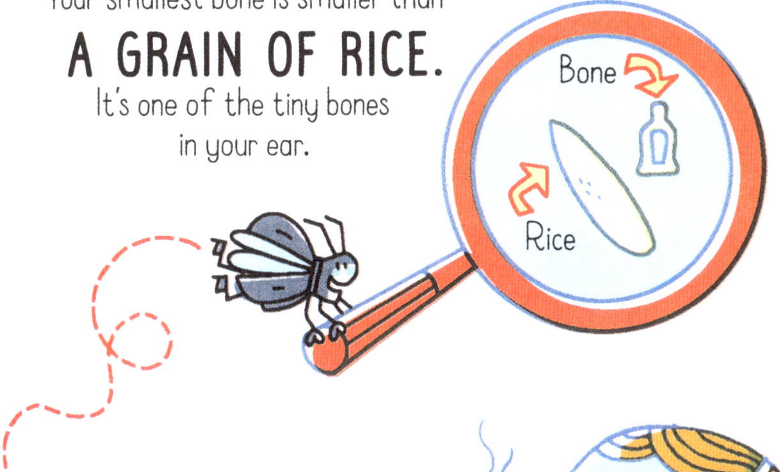

Bone

Rice

BLINK

You
BLINK
11,000
times a day.

Mmmm, sweet.

Your tongue can sense
FIVE MAIN TASTES
– sweet, sour, salty, bitter and 'umami' or savoury.

Your nose can detect around
A THOUSAND BILLION SMELLS.

Have a go at these little experiments to TEST your body.

Find your heart rate

You can time your heart using a stopwatch or clock.

1 Put your hand on your chest so you can feel your heart beating. (If you can't feel it there, try the side of your neck.)

2 Time a minute on your stopwatch, while counting how many beats you feel.

The number you get is called your HEART RATE.

3 Run around for a minute, then time your heart again. Has your heart rate changed?

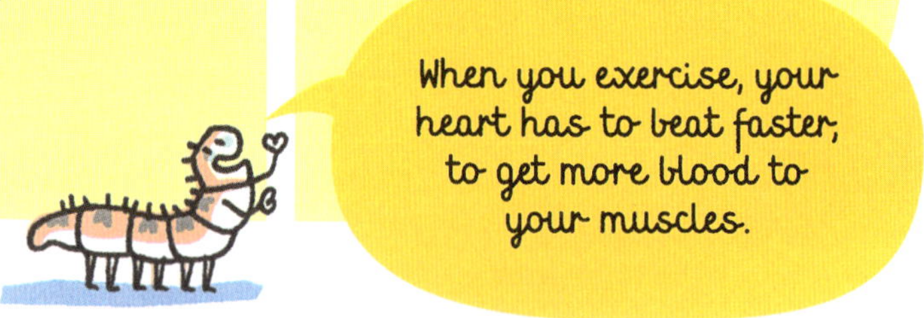

1...2...3...

When you exercise, your heart has to beat faster, to get more blood to your muscles.

Hear a heart

Doctors use a STETHOSCOPE to listen to people's hearts. You can make your own using just a cardboard tube and funnel. The tube from a roll of kitchen paper works well, and you might have a funnel in your kitchen.

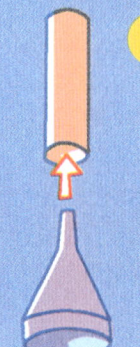

1 Put the thin end of the funnel inside the tube. Tape them together.

2 Gently hold the tube against a friend's chest, and put your ear to the funnel. Can you hear a heart beat?

How fast are you?

Test how quick your reactions are. All you need is a ruler and someone to help.

1. Hold out your hand like this.

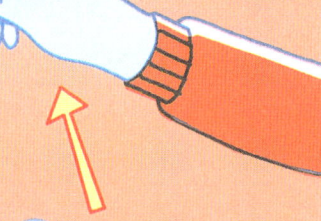

2. Ask your helper to hold a ruler just above your fingers, with 0 at the bottom.

3. Ask your helper to drop the ruler without warning. As soon as you see it fall, close your fingers and grab it.

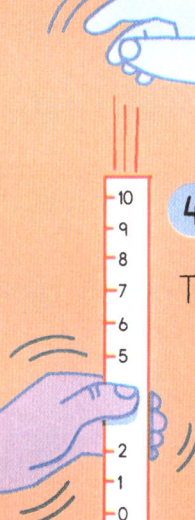

4. Check the number by your fingers. The smaller the number, the faster you were.

5. Repeat this a few times. Can you get faster?

Get dizzy

Spin in a circle 5 times. Can you stand on one leg afterwards?

Your balance comes from sensors inside your ears. Spinning around confuses them, so you feel dizzy.

Touch your nose

Close your eyes. Now try to touch your nose without looking. Can you do it?

Most people CAN do this, because your brain knows where your body parts are without seeing them.

Here is a whole skeleton. Each of the main bones is labelled with the scientific name doctors use, and the common name you might recognise.

You have tiny ear bones hidden inside your skull.

1. **CRANIUM** (SKULL)
2. **OSSICLES** (EAR BONES)
3. **MANDIBLE** (JAW)
4. **VERTEBRAL COLUMN** (SPINE)
5. **CLAVICLE** (COLLARBONE)
6. **SCAPULA** (SHOULDER BLADE)
7. **PHALANGES** (FINGER BONES)
8. **METACARPALS** (HAND BONES)
9. **CARPALS** (WRIST BONES)
10. & 11. **RADIUS** AND **ULNA** (LOWER ARM BONES)
12. **HUMERUS** (UPPER ARM BONE)
13. **RIBS**

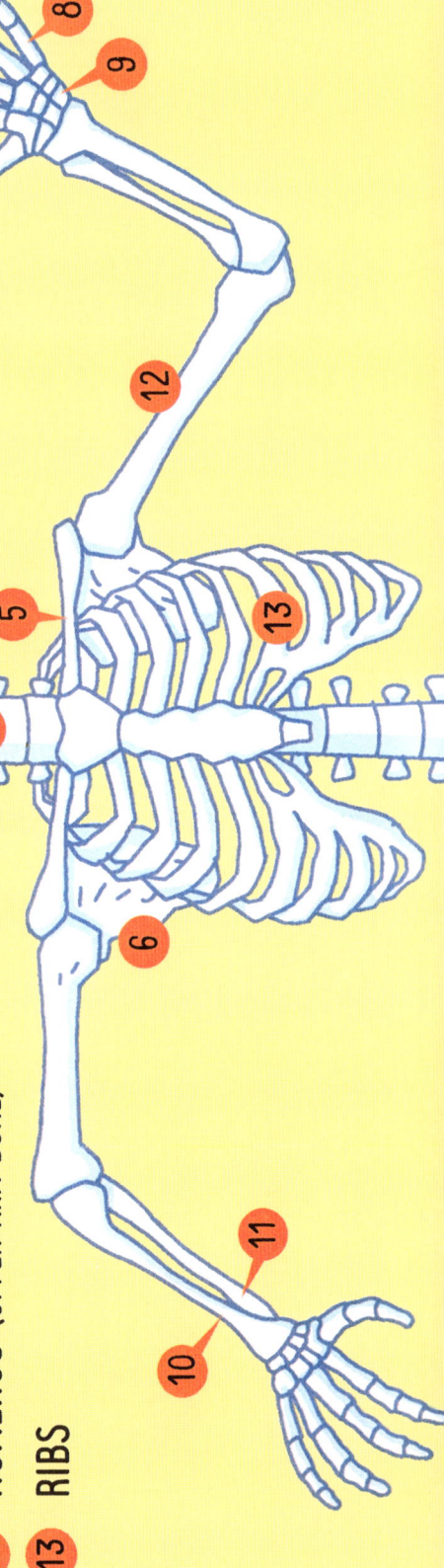

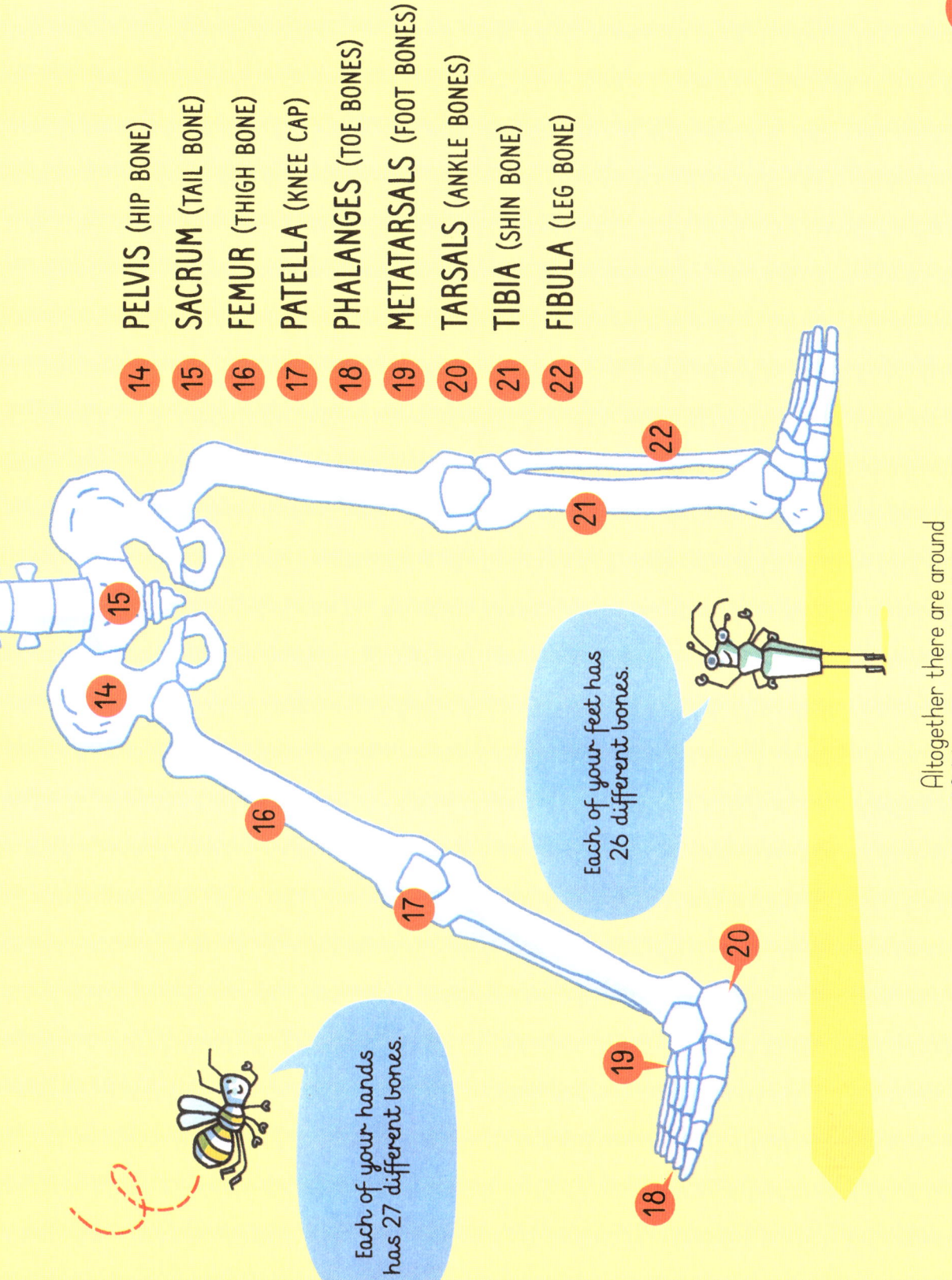

- 14 **PELVIS** (HIP BONE)
- 15 **SACRUM** (TAIL BONE)
- 16 **FEMUR** (THIGH BONE)
- 17 **PATELLA** (KNEE CAP)
- 18 **PHALANGES** (TOE BONES)
- 19 **METATARSALS** (FOOT BONES)
- 20 **TARSALS** (ANKLE BONES)
- 21 **TIBIA** (SHIN BONE)
- 22 **FIBULA** (LEG BONE)

Each of your feet has 26 different bones.

Each of your hands has 27 different bones.

Altogether there are around 206 bones in an adult skeleton.

An organ is a body part with a specific set of jobs. Here are all the organs described in this book.

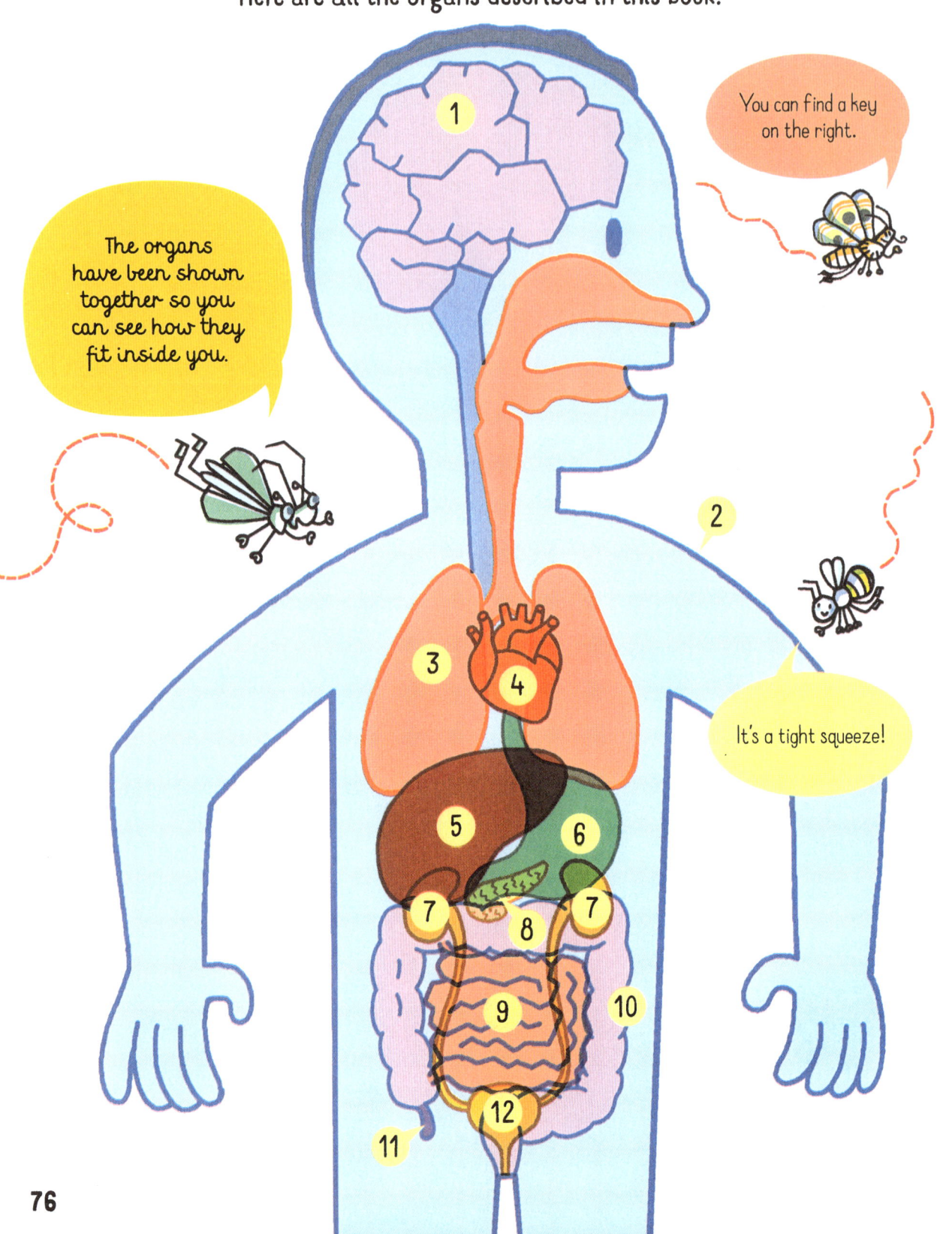

You can find a key on the right.

The organs have been shown together so you can see how they fit inside you.

It's a tight squeeze!

Doctors don't agree exactly how many organs you have, but there are at least 70.

These are some of the main ones.

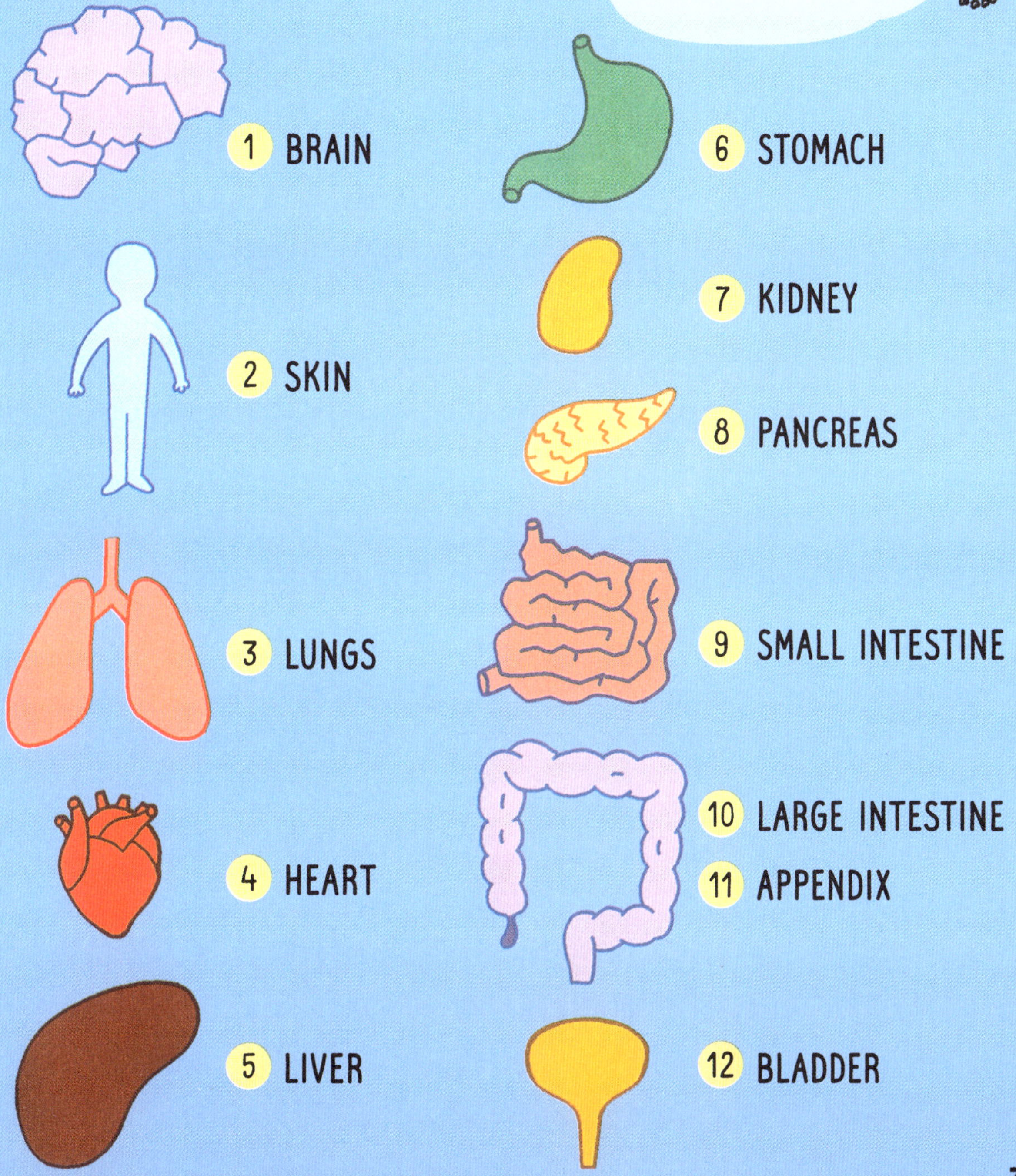

1. BRAIN
2. SKIN
3. LUNGS
4. HEART
5. LIVER
6. STOMACH
7. KIDNEY
8. PANCREAS
9. SMALL INTESTINE
10. LARGE INTESTINE
11. APPENDIX
12. BLADDER

Glossary

Here you can look up the meanings of some of the words in this book.

Allergy – a condition where your body reacts to something that is harmless to other people, such as pollen, dust or certain foods.

Antiseptic – a substance that kills **germs**.

Arteries – **blood vessels** that carry blood away from your heart.

Asthma – a condition where the tubes in your lungs get narrower, which can make it harder to breathe.

Bacteria – a type of tiny living thing. Some bacteria are harmless, many are helpful, but some can make you ill.

Blood vessels – tubes that carry blood around your body.

Bone marrow – a spongy substance in the middle of your bones.

Bruise – a dark mark made by blood leaking beneath your skin.

Capillaries – small **blood vessels** that join up **arteries** and **veins**.

Carbohydrate – a **nutrient** in food that gives you energy.

Cells – the tiny building blocks that make up every bit of your body. There are lots of types, for example: **red blood cells**, **white blood cells**, **platelets** and **nerve cells**.

Genes – the instructions that tell your body how to grow; they are found inside your **cells**.

Germs – tiny living things that can get inside your body and make you ill.

Joint – where two bones meet, for example your elbow or knee.

Melanin – a dark substance in your skin that helps to protect you from the sun.

Microbes – living things that are so tiny you need a microscope to see them.

Nerve cells – a type of **cell** that passes messages between your brain and your body.

Nutrients – substances in your food that you need to stay healthy, for example **carbohydrate** and **protein**.

Oxygen – a gas in the air that you need to breathe.

Platelets – spiky **cells** in your blood that help to form scabs.

Protein – a **nutrient** in food that helps your body to grow and repair itself.

Puberty – how your body changes as you turn into an adult.

Red blood cells – round **cells** in your blood that carry **oxygen**.

Sign language – a way of communicating using your hands and arms, rather than speaking.

Veins – **blood vessels** that carry blood back to your heart.

Virus – a type of **germ**.

White blood cells – **cells** in your blood that help to fight off illnesses.

X-rays – a way of seeing inside your body, often used to check if bones are broken.

Index

A
allergies 22, 60-61
arteries 17

B
babies 5, 41, 58-59, 62-64
bladder 24, 76-77
blood 16-19, 20-21, 24-25, 27, 54, 56, 58, 72
bones 26-27, 37, 46, 48, 59, 64, 70-71, 74-75
brain 26, 28-32, 36-37, 42-43, 51, 64-65, 70, 73, 76-77

C
calcium 46
cells 18-19, 54, 70

D
digesting 22-25, 47
drinking 7, 24-25, 55

E
eating 7, 22-23, 25, 34, 39, 46-47, 50, 61, 64, 66
exercise 19, 48-49, 72

F
families 66, 68-69
feelings 7, 29, 38-45, 48, 59
first aid 56-57
food 22-23, 25, 32, 46-47, 53, 60-61

G
genes 68-69
germs 10, 19, 50, 52-57
growing up 4, 7, 62-67

H
hair 4, 8, 12-13, 46, 53, 65, 68-69
hearing 6, 33, 35, 37-38, 67, 72
heart 16-19, 29, 43, 48-49, 71-72, 76-77
hospital 57-59

I
illnesses 47, 50, 52-59, 61
intestines 22-23, 25, 76-77

K
kidneys 24, 76-77

L
liver 25, 76-77
lungs 16-21, 48, 76-77

M
muscles 14-15, 20, 26, 70-71

N
nerves 28, 70

O
organs 24-25, 76-77

S
senses 6, 28-29, 32-37, 67, 71
sight 6, 29, 33-36, 47, 67
skeleton 26-27, 74-75
skin 4, 8-11, 46, 56-57, 76-77
sleep 31, 51
smell 6, 32, 34, 71
sound 33, 35, 37
stomach 22-23, 76-77

T
taste 32, 34, 71
touch 32, 34, 57, 73

V
veins 17
viruses 52
vitamins 47

W
washing 50, 53, 56, 59
water 22-24, 47, 50, 55, 57
windpipe 20-21

X
x-rays 59

Use this index to find out which pages things are mentioned on.